COUNTRY COOKERY

KATHLEEN THOMAS
COOKERY ADVISER
ELIZABETH DAVID

Drawings by Miriam Macgregor

TREASURE PRESS

For
Susanna, Simon and Victoria;
Emma and Sophie with love

First published in Great Britain as *West Country Cookery*
by B. T. Batsford Ltd

This edition published by Treasure Press
59 Grosvenor Street
London W 1
Reprinted 1984
© 1979 Kathleen Thomas
ISBN 0 90 7407 96 X
Printed in Czechoslovakia
50494/2

COUNTRY COOKERY

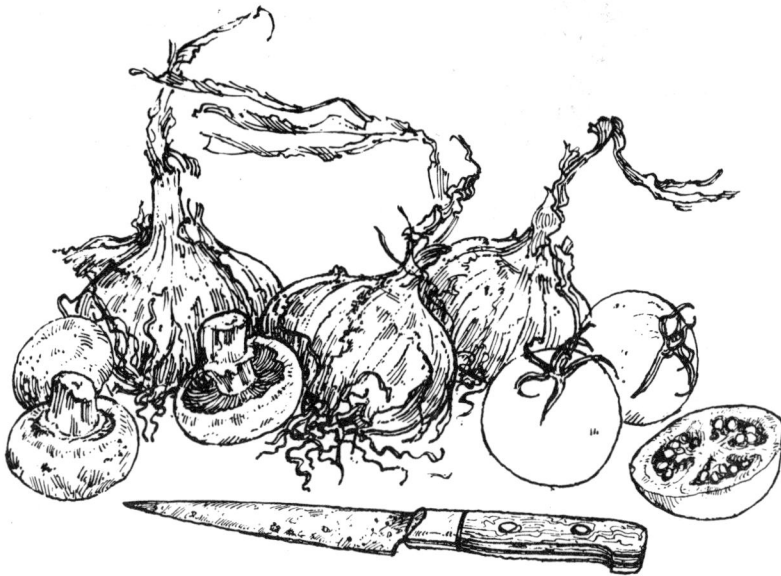

Contents

List of Illustrations

Acknowledgments

I should like to thank all those people who have helped with the making of this book, and in particular the Westminster Bank for permission to use information on cider-making from their *Bank Review* of November 1975; also F.W. Beech, of Long Ashton Research Station, for help on the making of cider, perry and mead; Messrs Devenish Breweries Weymouth for permission to quote them on the subject of real ale and traditional brewing; the editor of *Farmers Weekly* for permission to use many of the recipes sent me by readers during the time I wrote my weekly cookery column; and, lastly, all the people who so kindly sent me recipes and information as to where good food can still be bought in the West Country.

I should like to express my thanks to Elizabeth David for two reasons. First, for putting forward my name to the publishers as a possible author for this book, and secondly for being herself the author of the books on provincial cookery which first interested me in the cookery of my own country, which has been my enthralling study ever since.

I am also particularly indebted to Pamela Vandyke Price for letting me use her invaluable opinion on English wines. Pamela is Wine Correspondent of *The Times* and her knowledge of wines of all countries is incomparable.

Finally, my apologies to all those people whose names I have missed, and my thanks to all who helped me with information and a pleasant welcome. If this book has done nothing else, it has made me see more of the West Country and shown me that, next to my own native Yorkshire, the West Country has my heart.

For permission to reproduce the following photographs, the Author and Publishers would like to thank Exeter City Library (pp. 8 and 50); Priest's House Museum, Wimborne (pp. 68-9); Kenneth Scowen (frontispiece and pp. 62-3); J. Stevens-Cox (p. 35); Studio St. Ives Ltd. (p. 17); John Topham (pp. 41 and 76); the photograph on p. 135 is from the Publishers' own collection.

Introduction

I was born a daughter of Martha rather than of Mary: as a child I was perfectly happy to cook – with a variety of ingredients ranging from mud and water to porridge oats and sour milk (meant, I suspect, for the pigs next door) – and cook I did on a rusty little old stove in a disused outhouse. This outhouse was part of a long range of such buildings belonging to the Cotswold farmhouse my parents had taken, to begin with as a holiday home, and then, later, when my mother joined my father in India, as a permanent home for us children. The buildings were disused because we only lived in the house; the farm was still worked by a neighbouring farmer and in our garden wall stood a locked door through which we dare not penetrate,' . . . nice children don't play in farmyards.' But this was really the only prohibition laid on us, otherwise my brothers and I spent long hours, days even, roaming the cowslip decorated countryside, tunnelling into the 'cexy' (local name for all wild carrot and cow parsley plants) grass to make nests or caves for ourselves, and plodding the two miles of rutted country lanes which separated us from a family of cousins. And always I was the cook, the provider of or scrounger for food, in any form. Not that I can believe that we were hungry, but food always seemed a necessary part of the game we happened to be playing, and I always cooked it, gathered the wood for our fires, cleared up after everyone else . . . and I liked it. I still do.

I suppose it is this inherent taste for domesticity which colours my approach to, and fascination with, the social history of our foods – how they were cooked, who ate them, even who did the washing up. It is the people who lived in the farmhouses who interest me; what they grew, how they prepared it, ate it, stored it. It is the scenes of domesticated countryside which make my heart turn over – not the wild beauty of Exmoor but the small grey farmhouses in the valley with their buildings and fields which men have worked for hundreds of years; not the woods and copses of Dorset but the villages of whitewashed houses where people have lived since Domesday Book; not the fierce light of Bodmin Moor but the steep little streets leading down to the sea where fishermen have pulled in their boats and dried their nets over the long hard years.

The beauty of the chalk hills of Dorset lies, for me, in the fact that sheep graze there. The landscape stretching from Culmstock Beacon is a landscape of fields, hedgerows and small villages – people live in them, cows graze the fields, it is a man-made landscape. But its beauty comes from the fact that the men who made it were not aiming at beauty, they wanted usefulness;

and man very often achieves a greater beauty when usefulness is the first aim. The shining levels of the Glastonbury Marshes are evidence of men's work and lives. Men made the reames to carry water off the fields so that stock could graze there; they planted the willows on the banks to give shelter, not beauty, but what beauty they achieved.

Sir Henry Courtney, an eighteenth-century architect, said he liked his buildings to have 'commodity, firmness and delight'. Well, I like my landscape to have usefulness, order and delight; I hate to see deserted farmhouses, cottages which have outlived their owners or just become uneconomic to repair. A cottage near my home, deeply hidden in a wood, has become just such a ruin; only a few stone walls and an overgrown well can still be seen. It hurts me to feel that people once lived there and could have done so again if only it had not been left too late.

A new feeling is arising in the countryside and people are seeing how beautiful old buildings were, how well they fitted into the landscape, and restoration and conservation have become the new words. But the conservationists must beware of seeing the countryside as something wild and age old, kindly provided for their delectation; it isn't. At least two-thirds of our countryside is man-made, lovingly fashioned by the people who lived in it – the estate owners, the farmers, the smallholders and the cottagers. Left to itself, the countryside would rapidly become a tangle of briars and nettles, saplings and goosegrass. We have our wild places in the south-west – the moors and woods, the marshes and tracts of woodland – but it is the domestic landscapes which make it such a pleasant place to live. The conservationists who cry out for more wild places, more uncultivated stretches, must realize that it would not be half as pleasant if the people who live here did not look after it all the year round.

The West Country of England, on which this book is centred, is a place with little documentation; wars rarely happened here, plague and famine occasionally, flood fairly often—but nothing very earth-shaking or headline-making. The history books record, mostly, the simple life of ordinary people living by and off their land. You can read these books telling of events in this remote corner of England, and you will learn of what the people grew in their fields, but nowhere can you find how they cooked what they grew. You can read agricultural surveys which will give you the number of sheep and cattle, how they were reared, how fed and how slaughtered, but none of the books tell you how they were prepared for eating. You can search through architectural treatises about the sorts of buildings our ancestors inhabited, how they built them, the materials they used—you can read about cruck-roofed houses, screen passages, cob and thatch and stone—but nowhere do you find more than a passing mention of the hearthstone or the bread oven, the fires of peat or the use of sea coal. In all the volumes of G.M. Trevelyan's *Social History of England* there are not, all told, more than twenty pages or so telling how the inhabitants of England cooked their food. Even descriptions of mediaeval banquets don't make it clear how the kitchen serfs produced the delicacies described when all they appear to have had were open fires and the slow-to-heat bread oven. And in any case the banquets were presumably for the gentry; how did the poor cook?

Hobbes described the lives of the poor as 'nasty, brutish and short' and there must have been many years when this could truthfully have been said of the lives of the peasants and small farmers of the West Country. Only Bristol, Exeter and Plymouth, and some of the Dorset wool towns and the small ports which thrived on the fishing trade ever generated much wealth; even the 'great' houses were fairly few and far between. It is tempting to imagine that the rural poor were never quite so deprived as the urban poor—the people of the mines, the looms and the nail-making hovels—but life must have been hard and thankless when bad winters took the cattle and late springs brought little hope.

Beer, barley and bacon are said to have been the staples of the diet throughout the country before imports of more exotic foods came from other lands (though in the south-west we should probably substitute cider for beer) and certainly bacon played a most important part in the diet of the cottager or farm worker. It was only the lord of the manor or the abbot of a monastery who could call on the pigeons from the dovecot or venison from the forest.

The importance of pigeons in the West Country diet is reflected in the numerous recipes for 'squab pie' which used the young pigeons before they could fly. One monastery day book records the killing of more than 20,000 young pigeons in one year both for their own use and for sale. The venison, of course, would have been eaten fresh or well hung. Hannah Glasse in her *The Art of Cookery Made Plain and Easy* (1772) says that venison can be hung in a good game larder for upwards of two months'. Fynes Moryson, a most prolific traveller, writing shortly after the death of Queen Elizabeth I, says, 'In the seasons of the year the English eat fallow deer plentifully, as bucks in summer and does in winter, which they bake in pasties, and this venison pasty is a dainty rarely found in any other kingdom'. And he goes on, 'The English inhabitants eat almost no flesh commoner than hens, and for geese they eat them in two seasons, when they are fatted upon the stubble after harvest and when they are green in Whitsuntide', though this doesn't agree with my own information about green geese which is that they were the ones eaten about September. Perhaps he was a little prejudiced, as he continues, 'They also have a great plenty of conies (rabbits) the flesh thereof is fat tender and more delicate than any I have eaten in other parts, the German conies are more like roasted cats than the English conies'.[1]

This sounds to be good living yet less than fifty years earlier Harrison says, 'The bread throughout the land is made of such grain as the soil yieldeth, the gentility commonly provide themselves sufficiently of wheat for their own tables, while the household and poor neighbours in some shires are forced to content themselves with rye or barley yea and in some times of dearth many with bread made of beans, peason or oats and some acorns among'.[2] But still neither of these writers, you will notice, says how the food was *cooked*.

Perhaps the pictures in the Bayeux Tapestry tell us most. Here the cooks are shown boiling a pot over one fire, roasting at another and then serving the result on the spits on which it has been cooked. Five hundred years later we read of that intrepid traveller Celia Fiennes, on a riding tour of the West Country, who found her supper at Penzance 'boiling on a fire always supplied with bush of furze as that is to be the only fuel to dress a joint of meat or broth'.[3] though this was largely because the natural forests of the West Country had been cut down for building and fuel and sea coal had not as yet reached the region.

Turner's *Domestic Architecture*, dated 1311, gives the contents of a country-house larder as 'the carcases of twenty oxen and fifteen pigs, of herrings eight thousand, of dograves seven score, twenty pounds of almonds, thirty of rice, six barrels of lard, enough oatmeal to last to Easter and two quarters of salt', but this, you must remember, was a rich man's larder; that of the common man was more likely to contain 'a pig salted, a barrel half-full of lard, some fish salted [carp perhaps?], some barley meal and a sack of wheaten flour, and a quarter of salt'.[4] With such scanty knowledge as we have it is unsafe to generalize about the diet of the poorer people, and even the description of banquets placed before the lord of the manor does not tell us very much—it is certain that they did not live always like this, and we can only surmise what meals were like by picking up scraps of information as they come our way.

Probably here in the south-west the rural poor, living nearer the soil, fared rather better than others in more populated areas, except in times of real famine. But there is not much evidence of high living, except at certain

[1]Fynes Moryson
[2]William Harrison
[3]Celia Fiennes
[4]Marjorie and C.H.B. Quennell

times in history when, for instance, Bath was the focal point of so many routes—routes which took the rich produce of the west to the towns where the money was. In the eighteenth century, Welsh mutton, Somerset cider, clotted cream from the dairy farms of Somerset, fish from the River Severn, salmon, fresh trout, pilchards and sea fish from the Cornish fishing fleets, these all came by the coastal route, but Bristol and Bath were the great meeting points and redistribution centres of all this wealth and I suspect that this is the picture that many of us still carry in our minds when we think of the West Country.

In many centuries this picture of richness and variety would not have been true, and I am afraid that today we have come to accept a creeping uniformity about our food. You are as likely to be offered a mass-produced fruit pie just unwrapped from its highly decorated carton as you are the 'apple pie in a deep dish, on top of which they laid a cover of custard which they told me they made from the cream only . . . it was the best dish I had ever tasted' as wrote Celia Fiennes when touring on her 'sure-footed little horse'.

But local skills are not yet all lost; good cooks still ply their trade, even if you do have to search out their products, and to make this book more interesting and useful to the reader I have given at the end a directory of at least a selection of the places in the West Country where good local foods can be bought. This is not, I realize, a definitive list, but in my travels through the four counties I have searched out small bakeries and butcher's shops, farmhouse cheese-makers, dairy stalls at markets, the people who actually make the foods and the shops where you can buy them. I apologize to those whose names I have missed, and I would suggest to the reader who is looking for good, home-made, locally produced food that he or she asks in any small town or village for the baker who makes crusty bread, the butcher who sells his own sausages, the home-made cake shop and the farm or market garden where they sell fresh-picked fruit, crisp lettuces or sun-warmed tomatoes. You may have to spend some time searching, but it will be well worth it in the end.

Note on metrication
The recipes in this book give both metric and imperial quantities. However, the metric quantities are not exact conversions but are adjusted to give equally successful results. It is important, therefore, to follow either all-metric or all-imperial measurements and not to mix the two.

Fish and Shellfish

Fish and Shellfish

The West Country with its long coastal stretches has always been famous for its fish. Poor agriculturally and economically as the region had always been, the wealth of its fishing has been almost its only natural resource. The pilchard industry at Plymouth is mentioned as early as 1378. Clovelly and Lynmouth have been noted for their herrings since 1630 and the Cornish pilchard industry gave rise to the famous Stargazy pie. It is one of the tragedies of modern economics that today the fishing industry has been replaced by the plying of boats for hire by the summer visitor, which, though a useful function, is a poor substitute for the vigour of the life of the old trade. And as I write, the industry is being hit by a new storm; the battle of the fishing limits is still unresolved and doubts are added to by the large numbers of vessels coming into the grounds from other parts of our coasts and from other countries.

The fish of the West Country have always been sharply divided into the coastal fish—pilchards, herrings, mackerel—the shellfish such as crabs, lobsters, cockles, and, the aristocrats of all fish cooking, the trout and the salmon taken from the little trout streams and the great salmon rivers. Severn salmon is thought by some people to be of a better flavour than any other. The peasant population would have been consumers of the first sort of fish, while the lord of the manor, who owned most of the freshwater fishing rights, ate the trout and the salmon (though I daresay a few have always been poached both in past times and today).

Then you may also find small catches of fish like bream and crayfish which used to be caught in the lower reaches of the Exe. If you are holidaying in the south-west you should look out for the blackboard placed on the pier or foreshore of many of the fishing towns and villages, saying 'Selling (at X o'clock)', which means that the catch will be sold from a boat as it comes in and you can make your way to where the crowd has gathered when you will get the chance to buy fish so fresh that nothing will ever taste the same again.

This is really the only way to buy mackerel, and if you can get them straight from one of the boats you should take them only as far as necessary to build a wood fire, then wrap the fish in buttered greaseproof paper and bury them in the embers of the fire until the oil begins to run. They'll 'need no sauce but hunger', as Huck Finn so rightly said. Some people maintain that they taste even better if you have caught them yourself, but I am too old to test the theory. The trouble with mackerel, as with many other good things, is that you quickly tire of a surfeit, and then the question remains what to do with the rest of the pile of fish you have so optimistically bought? In the recipe section I have given one solution to this by way of pickling. But be warned: mackerel do not freeze well.

Of course, it doesn't take much imagination to see that vast catches of fish do not do the local fishermen any good, and on occasion fish have to be sold for fish manure at much lower prices. So I was delighted to find that in the little hamlet of Charlestown, a suburb (if it can be called that) of St Austell, an enterprising businessman has set up Cornish Smoked Fish Ltd. In a small grey cluster of buildings in this little Cornish fishing village (whose business seems largely to be making a turn-round point for enormous lorries from the china clay industry which come to discharge their

cargoes into waiting barges) you can see huge vats of mackerel waiting to be smoked and turned into what could be the answer to the smoked salmon and trout dilemma, that of being priced out of the market. The little (average 110g or 6 oz) fish which this company is turning out are delicious as a starter or served with salads as a main course. They are now also experimenting with a smoked mackerel pâté, for which I wish them all success; but if you want to make your own I have included a simple recipe for Potted Mackerel.

Pilchards probably come first in importance of the sea-water catches, though fishermen will tell you that the English do not care for the humble pilchard, and much of the catch goes abroad. Called, romantically, 'fair maids of Cornwall', this name is merely a corruption from *fumade* which comes from the Spanish word 'to smoke'. However, pilchards can claim to be the basis of what is probably the most romantically named of all local dishes, the famous Stargazy Pie, though I fear that most modern stomachs turn queasy at the notion of it. There was a certain amount of sense behind the traditional method of preparing this dish because oily fish are really tastier if cooked with their heads on, but I cannot see a modern consumer being enamoured by the idea of seeing a circle of fish heads with eyes gazing at him from a plate. But to encourage you to discover the excellence of pilchards I have included in the recipes my own method for an open flan using pilchards which can be eaten hot or cold and, just for the fun of the thing, I've put in the old traditional recipe as well.

No West Country cookery book would be complete without at least a mention of elvers. The elver is an immature eel and can still be found, by those who know, in parts of the Bristol Channel and the rhynes (or reames) of Somerset. If you want to taste them, then the only way is to get into the good graces of some of the local people who still fish for elvers with almost religious fervour. Dorothy Hartley tells how they do it.

> The elver shoal itself looks like a mass of jelly swimming in the water; it consists of millions of elvers, and can best be described as transparent spaghetti. The fish are caught by dipping them out of the rhynes in scoops made of cloth, or buckets and pans, as any net would let the fish through. They are washed in running water and then cooked at once. As soon as the transparent mass touches the hot pan or fat, it turns opaque (exactly as white of egg becomes opaque and visible). It is stirred and turned till it is all evenly cooked, and eaten with salt and pepper and bread and butter. It is best hot, cooked loosely, like whitebait (though never so crisp), but the marsh folk also make 'elver cake', which is the same mass of fish, seasoned with chopped herbs (a suspicion of onion

and butter or bacon-fat added), and the whole turned into a dish, and pressed down till set and cold. This elver cake then turns out and can be cut in slices.

I doubt whether there is much future for them; a local hotelier says he puts elvers on his menu whenever they are available but only the occasional diner is brave enough to sample them.

A particularly welcome development is the growth in fishing waters and the consequent greater availability of fishing in reservoirs and canals as well as rivers. Certainly most of these yield only coarse fish such as tench, bream and chubb—none of them, in my opinion, edible—but the dedicated fisherman doesn't fish for the pot and most of the catch is thrown back. I suspect, too, that many of the men who sit silently on the banks of the broad straight river Parret or of one of the Bristol reservoirs enjoy the sheer peace of the reflections in the still water as much as the thrill of the catch.

Not for them the glories of the salmon or trout, although once the story was quite different. All local history books quote the tale of the apprentices of Exeter who rebelled at the fact that they had to eat salmon 'twice weekly', and the monks of one Dorset monastery complained that their stewpond contained 'nothing but trout'.

Some determined efforts are now being made to 'farm' trout and spectacular claims are made for certain breeding and feeding methods which are said to result in huge fish of salmon-like proportions. The salmon itself, I am glad to say, defies all efforts at improvement in this way and all that the water bailiffs can do is assist its passage up the salmon 'leaps' and guard it against the nightly prowlings of the now-armed gangs of poachers.

The fishing rights on rivers in the south-west can increasingly be sold or let for phenomenal sums quite unrelated to the value of the fish in them—but fishermen will always pay for their sport. The salmon is certainly a noble fish, but for myself I ask nothing better than a small fat brown trout from my own stream—the beautiful, peaceful, sometimes secret, river Culm—which rises at Culmhead and flows down its valley through Hemyock, Culmstock, Uffculme and on to Cullompton, finally to join the Exe. Cows graze beside it, kingfishers flash over it, herons stalk its banks, and the little fat brown trout breed in its pools. A travel writer once called it 'the loveliest small river in England': who am I to disagree?

SHELLFISH

Crab-on-the-Cobb

50g (2 oz) butter
50g (2 oz) flour
575ml (1 pint) milk
,salt
black pepper
225g (½ lb.) crab meat
4 slices toast from large loaf,
   hot-buttered
celery slivers for garnish

This is an old family name from 70 years ago when the crab was always bought fresh on the Cobb at Lyme Regis during summer holidays.

Make a thick white sauce from the butter, flour and milk and season well. Add the crab meat, turn into a bowl or mortar and pound the mixture until it is thoroughly amalgamated (the sauce and crab will not mix properly unless they are pounded).

Pile the crab onto the toast and serve very hot garnished with celery slivers.

serves 4

Devilled Crab

100g (¼ lb.) fresh breadcrumbs
25g (1 oz) soft butter
2 tablespoons top of milk
½ cup hot water
1 teaspoon Worcester sauce
½ teaspoon dry mustard
salt
black pepper
225g (½ lb.) crab meat
2 tablespoons dry breadcrumbs
   (optional)

Mix together all the ingredients except the crab meat and dry breadcrumbs in a saucepan, beating until the butter is creamy. Simmer gently, then stir in the crab meat and turn the mixture into a well-buttered pie-dish. Dry breadcrumbs can be strewn on top to form a crust.

Bake at 180°C (350°F, Gas Mark 4) for about 20 minutes until golden. Chopped stuffed olives are a good accompaniment to this dish.

serves 6

Cockle Pie

150ml (¼ pint) cockles per
   person
150ml (¼ pint) milk per
   person
1 teaspoon anchovy essence
   per person
butter for sauce
flour for sauce
salt
black pepper

Scald the cockles and as they open transfer them to the milk. When all the cockles are ready and have sat in the milk for a few minutes, drain them and set the milk aside for the sauce.

Make the sauce using butter and flour as for a white sauce, adding the anchovy to the milk and seasoning well with salt, pepper and nutmeg.

Butter a 1-litre (2 pint) pie dish and dust with a little pepper, followed by a layer of breadcrumbs. Dot tiny pieces of butter over the crumbs and cover with a layer of cockles. Pour over a layer of sauce, then more crumbs, butter, cockles and another layer of sauce.

nutmeg
1 small cupful brown
   breadcrumbs per person
150mg (2 oz) mashed potato per
   person
1 lemon wedge per person

Continue until the dish is almost full and all these ingredients are used up, finishing with a layer of sauce. Cover with a thin crust of mashed potato and bake in a moderate oven 180°C (350°F, Gas Mark 4) for half an hour. Serve hot with wedges of lemon.

Crayfish

To prepare the crayfish they must first be dropped in boiling water for a few minutes, when they will turn pink. The meat is then picked from the shells.

To serve: the shelled fish may be added to any green salad and tossed in a plain oil and vinegar or lemon juice dressing (in 3 to 1 proportions) seasoned with salt and pepper. Allow 100g (¼ lb.) fish per portion.

Alternatively, the fish may be heated in a foundation white sauce (allowing 150ml (¼ pint) sauce per 100g (¼ lb.) fish for one serving), to which a little cream may profitably be added, seasoned with cayenne and salt and flavoured with a little anchovy sauce. Turn this mixture into deep scallop shells, cover with breadcrumbs, sprinkle with a little melted butter and brown in a hot oven or under a pre-heated grill.

FISH

Grilled Mackerel

2 small mackerel
salt
cayenne pepper
maître d'hôtel butter
2 quarters of lemon
parsley to garnish

Cut off the heads and fins and make two deep cuts diagonally across either side of the fish.

Cook the fish on a well-greased rack either over a hot, clear fire or under a pre-heated grill, turning after 12–15 minutes to brown the second side for about the same length of time.

Season with salt and a little cayenne and serve immediately accompanied by the butter and lemon and garnished with parsley.

If available, a little finely chopped fresh tarragon may be worked into the butter.

serves 2

Marinated Mackerel

4 mackerel
1 onion, finely chopped
sprig of thyme, chopped
6 cloves
10 peppercorns
2 bay leaves, chopped
2 teaspoons salt
blade of mace
425ml (¾ pint) vinegar
   (approx.)

Clean and prepare the mackerel and arrange them in a pie-dish. Sprinkle over the onion, thyme, cloves, peppercorns, bay leaves and salt. Add the mace and pour over sufficient vinegar to cover well.

Bake, uncovered, in a moderate oven, 190°C (375°F, Gas Mark 5) for 40 or 50 minutes. When the fish are cooked, remove them from the liquid, arrange on a serving dish and strain the liquor over them. Serve cold.

serves 4

Pickled Mackerel

'Take six large mackerel and cut them into round pieces. Then take an ounce [25g] of beaten pepper, three large nutmegs, a little mace, and a handful of salt. Mix your salt and beaten spice together, then make two or three holes in each piece, and with your finger thrust the seasoning into the holes. Rub the pieces all over with the seasoning, fry them brown in oil, and let them stand till they be cold. Then put them into vinegar and cover them with oil. They are delicious eating, an' they be well covered, they will keep a long time.'[2]

Potted Mackerel

Butter the inside of an earthenware crock, including the lid which should be well-fitting. Place in it slices of raw, boned mackerel, together with a few peppercorns, salt, a pinch of mace and allspice to taste (quantities depending on the amount of fish being potted). Add some good fish stock to about 2½ cm (1 inch) in depth to prevent burning. Cover with buttered greaseproof paper and a weight before putting on the lid.

Cook for at least an hour in a moderate oven, 180°C (350°F, Gas Mark 4), and after cooking leave the fish to cool in the crock.

Remove the fish when cold and drain well. Remove any skin and stray bones, add more salt and pepper if necessary and pound the flesh in a mortar with a little clarified butter. Press through a fine sieve and put into small pots, covering each with a thin layer of clarified butter. Store in a cool place.

Serve with hot toast and wedges of lemon.

[2]*Cornish Recipes*

Traditional Stargazy Pie

This pie should be made with pilchards, but herring or mackerel can be used instead. The pastry cover derives from the idea of the pasty and made it possible for the worker to carry the fish easily to his place of work. The old recipes recommended that the head should not be covered, though it must be kept on to conserve the juices.

Slit and gut the fish, removing small fins and wiping off the scales. Season well and put a spoonful of finely chopped onion and green herbs into the cavity (this improves the flavour and keeps the fish moist while baking). The stuffing can be varied with a spoonful of mustard, pummace from the cider press, pickled samphire, or a plain crumb-and-herb filling, but it should be kept moist.

Prepare enough plain shortcrust pastry to make a fairly thin base and a thicker top crust for the dish you are using. Roll out the base, line the dish and lay the fish on the pastry with the heads pointing outwards. Cover with the top crust (leaving the heads uncovered if desired), pressing the pastry down around each fish to make separate pasties. Brush over the tops with a little saffroned milk and beaten egg to give a golden colour.

Bake in a moderate oven, 190°C (375°F, Gas Mark 5), until nicely browned. Each fish can be cut separately from the pie.

Open Stargazy Pie

225g (½ lb.) shortcrust pastry (approx.)
225g (½ lb.) pilchards, mackerel or herring, cooked and flaked
2 hard-boiled eggs, diced
1 cupful fresh breadcrumbs
1 cupful top of milk or single cream
salt
black pepper
pinch thyme and marjoram (optional)
6 stuffed olives, very thinly sliced

This is my own, modern variation on Stargazy Pie..

Line an 20-cm (8-inch) flan case with the pastry. Mix together the fish, eggs, breadcrumbs, milk, seasoning and herbs and leave the mixture to stand for about 10 minutes.

Press the fish mixture into the flan case, smoothing over the top, and decorate with the olive slices, which will look a little like fish eyes but not so much so as to be repellent to modern taste!

serves 6-8

Marinated Pilchards

Allow two or three pilchards per person.

Clean the fish, washing each one very thoroughly inside, and put a bay leaf inside each, with plenty of pepper and salt. Arrange the fish in an enamel or glazed earthenware dish and pour on enough vinegar to cover the fish. Cover with a lid or tie on a sheet of greaseproof paper securely. Bake at 150°C (300°F, Gas Mark 2) for about 20–25 minutes until the bones of the fish are completely soft. Serve cold.

Mackerel and herring can be prepared in the same way.

Dippy

6 pilchards
150ml (¼ pint) thin cream
675g (1½ lb.) potatoes, peeled
    and diced
salt
black pepper

Clean the fish, then simmer them in the cream with the potatoes and seasoning, in a covered pan, until soft.

serves 3

Steamed Salmon

Salmon is best cooked very simply. To steam, wrap the whole fish, or portion of the fish, in greased paper and lay it above fast-boiling water until cooked, allowing 15–20 minutes per 450g (1 lb.).

Slide the fish gently out of the water, remove the paper carefully and serve on a hot dish with its own broth (the juices inside the paper).

A small bouquet of herbs may be laid on the dish underneath the fish to give aroma, but do not over-season. Serve plainly, but if a sauce is to accompany this dish, it is usually fennel.

Roast Salmon

1) An old method of roasting salmon: season the cut of salmon with nutmeg and salt, stick with a few cloves and put one or two buttered bay leaves inside with a little spray of rosemary.

Roast at 155 - 160°C (315-325°F, Gas Mark 2½-3) allowing 20 minutes per 450g (1 lb.) and basting with butter. For a sauce, add to the gravy a very little vinegar, extra butter and thin slices of orange.

2) For a piece of salmon to be used cold with mayonnaise next day: season the fish, wrap it in buttered paper and enclose in a covered pot so that it is completely sealed. Bake at 155–160°C (315-325°F, Gas Mark 2½-3) allowing 20 minutes per 450g (1 ib.). Leave the pot unopened in a cool larder until just before serving next day, when it will be found in a pool of rich gravy and the meat very delicate and juicy.

All fish to be eaten cold is good cooked in this way as it retains the juice and flavour.

Fried Trout

For really small fish—say 100g (¼ lb) and smaller—there is only one satisfactory method: having cleaned and wiped them, dust inside with a little pepper and salt and fry them in any good fat (butter is best) until crisp.

Larger fish may be split open, the backbone removed, and fried as above; or they may be dipped in oatmeal, Scots fashion, and fried in a little butter or dripping. In either case serve hot with either plain melted butter or a *maître d'hôtel* sauce.

Grilled Trout

Suitable for fish up to or over 450g (1 lb.).

Clean the fish, open it out flat and remove the backbone; wipe dry and dust with pepper (but not salt which has a tendency to splutter in the eyes of the cook).

Fix the fish in a folding gridiron and grill, flesh to the fire, for about ten minutes. Turn, baste with a little melted butter, and finish cooking skin side down for a further ten minutes, sprinkling on some salt at the last moment. (With rainbow trout the basting is not necessary as providence has provided them with sufficient oil.)

The best fire for this method of cooking is a good wood fire which has ceased to blaze; but if it is necessary to cook the fish under an electric or gas grill, the order must be reversed —finishing the cooking with the flesh side towards the fire. The important point is that the skin must be underneath during the second part of the cooking.

Poultry
and Eggs

Poultry and Eggs

I doubt if anything in agricultural life has changed more in the past fifty years than poulty-keeping. The days of the farmer's wife with her few chickens from which she 'made' the housekeeping money are long gone, never to return, in spite of those who cry out for free-range eggs and deplore the fate of the battery hen.

However, the truth which these people will never face is that free-range hens simply don't produce eggs in the short, cold dark days of winter and we, the consumers of eggs, would have to go without fresh eggs for at least six months of the year instead of, as now, having a plentiful supply of fresh, firm-shelled, brown or white eggs all the year round. However nostalgically we may view pictures of a bustling farmer's wife, preferably in a sun-bonnet and clogs, scattering grain from a picturesque wooden skip to a flock of hungry hens, the reality of a large, heated, well-lit, deep-litter house with clean water and food always available is the one which provides the eggs we need. And the plentiful supply of young tender chickens means that a chicken in every pot is a luxury no longer, though some of us may hanker after a good old-fashioned boiler.

If someone were to write the history of the last hundred years of poultry-keeping, it would almost be the history of a hundred years of farm life as well. The backyard hen, the hen yard, the barn door fowl - all these phrases crop up in old farming books, and it was always the farmer's wife who managed the flock. She sat the eggs under a broody (still known, when we came to Devon 25 years ago, as a 'clocker'), fed the little chicks when they hatched, collected the eggs, took them to market and pocketed the egg money. And I must confess that there is nothing quite so soporific as a warm farmyard with a few contented hens scratching in the dust, nor anything quite as exciting as looking for a hen which has stolen her nest, as they say, and laid away under some hedge or a well-strawed corner of an old dark barn. But then, conversely, there is nothing quite so dismal as bedraggled hens shivering under an old cart with the rain streaming from their tail feathers, or finding the stolen nest only when the eggs have addled — nostalgia doesn't really pay!

So new ideas came to poultry-keeping: arks which penned the birds on the stubble or the grass and were moved every day leaving long green streaks where the hens had manured the ground, and giving splendid laying yields until the weather turned bad; then arks yielded to batteries - which caged the birds entirely and fed and watered them automatically - or deep-litter houses, huge ventilated sheds with shavings or other litter in which the birds clucked contentedly whatever the outside weather.

But we still have, too, the free-range hen beloved of some people who swear that nothing tastes like an egg from a hen ranging on grass and who will drive for miles to obtain such eggs. I hope it will not spoil their enjoyment when I say that some farmers have been known to put up a notice advertising 'Free-range eggs' and, cunningly, to keep a few hens on a patch of grass by the farm gate, but then to bolt round to the back of the buildings to collect the eggs from a deep-litter house well out of sight.

As with eggs, the marketing of poultry has been taken out of the hands of the farmer's wife. No more do you see, in any country town pannier market, a countrywoman with a few dressed poultry laid out on a clean cloth drawn over a trestle table. The modern farmer's wife is more likely to be sitting behind a well-ordered farm office desk doing the accounts with the aid of an electronic calculator, and I for one am glad that it should be so.

Geese, however, have always been a feature of West Country farming, and are still, although it is more and more difficult to buy one at Christmas. As many women balk — I do myself — at the idea of all that plucking, farmers sell to the big dealers instead. Old cookery books usually distinguish between Michaelmas geese and green geese, and it was only when we came to Devon that I found out the reason. Geese are grazing animals and a green goose is one that has been feeding off grass, while the Michaelmas goose (which is also called a goose from the stubble) is one from a flock which has been turned out to graze the stubble after the corn is cut, and these flocks also cleared up the grass which grew after the corn had been harvested. The bird will, of course, pick up the split grain as well as the grass and are as fat as butter by the end of the season. Today most geese are hand-fed for the Christmas trade.

Turkeys, though also the province of the big producer, are still bred by the farmer's wife in small flocks to supplement her Christmas money, and it is quite usual to hear someone making the rounds to ask for help at plucking time to make up bands of pluckers who then work furiously hard for a few days.

The turkey trade at Christmas has always had its pitfalls, mostly due to over-production by the commercial breeders, and although great efforts have been made to persuade us all to eat a turkey at Easter or any other holiday, the campaign has never made much headway. To be honest, the small turkey is a waste of money – there is too much carcass to the weight of meat - and the best turkey of all is one of 18 lb. or over, when there really is something to cut into.

POULTRY

Pot Roasted Fowl

one 1½-1¾kg (3½-4 lb.)
   boiling fowl
seasoned flour
4 slices fat bacon
2 cups chopped vegetables as
   available (onions, carrots,
   turnips, etc.)
100g (¼ lb.) mushrooms
a pinch of mixed herbs
1 cup stock or water

Joint the bird and dust with seasoned flour. Lay the bacon over the bottom of a heavy pan, add the vegetables and then pack in the chicken joints. Add the mushrooms and herbs and the liquid. Cover the pan tightly and cook over a very low heat (the contents of the pan should just sizzle quietly, no more) allowing about 15 minutes per 450g (1 lb.) weight of chicken—the flesh should be coming away from the bones by the end of the cooking time.

Serve either straight from the pot or arrange on a hot serving dish.

serves 8

Roast Boiling Fowl

one 1½-1¾kg (3½-4 lb.)
   boiling fowl
350-450g (¾-1 lb.) potatoes
   diced small
4 rashers fat bacon

Stuff the body cavity of the bird as full as possible with the potatoes. Cover the breast with bacon, wrap the whole fowl tightly in cooking foil and cook in a moderate oven, 190°C (375°F, Gas Mark 5), basting occasionally, for 2 – 2½ hours.

The secret of this method is that the steam from the potatoes keeps the flesh moist. They can be kept and used later for soup.

serves 8

September Pie

450g (1 lb.) boned, cooked
   chicken
flour for coating
100g (¼ lb.) mushrooms,
   sliced
2 onions, chopped
100g (¼ lb.) bacon, chopped
dripping for frying
flour for roux
275ml (½ pint) chicken stock
salt
pepper
225g (½ lb.) flaky pastry
egg to glaze

This recipe comes from an old unpublished West Country rectory 'Cookery Collection' lent to me by a friend from Tiverton.
Dice the chicken and lightly flour the pieces. Fry the mushrooms, onions and bacon in dripping until just golden, drain and remove from the fat. Next fry the chicken (adding a little more dripping if necessary), drain well, mix it with the vegetables and bacon and turn into a 1-litre (2-pint) pie dish.

Add enough flour to the fat in the frying pan to make a roux. Add the stock and bring to the boil, stirring well. Season and pour over the chicken mixture in the dish. Close with a pastry lid, brush over with egg and cook in a hot oven, 230°C (450°F, Gas Mark 8), for 35 minutes.

serves 4

Dorset Grilled Chicken

one 1-1½kg (2½-3 lb.)
    chicken, halved
1 lemon, *one* half only squeezed
    of juice
75g (3 oz) butter (approx)
salt
2 rashers streaky bacon, cut in
    narrow strips
50 g (2 oz) mushrooms, sliced
watercress for garnish
potato crisps for garnish

I was given this recipe by a Dorchester farmer's wife who said, 'So many of the regional chicken recipes are for using old or older birds, but now we only cook the small 1 -1½kg (2½ - 3 lb.) bird so this method may be of interest.'

Rub the chicken with the unsqueezed half of lemon. Melt 50g (2 oz) of the butter in a small pan and brush generously all over the chicken; then sprinkle with salt.

Lay the chicken halves, skin side down, in a grill pan with the rack removed. Cook slowly for 12–15 minutes, basting frequently; then turn and grill the other side for a further 12–15 minutes, still basting (adding more butter if necessary). When cooked, the skin should be crisp and golden and if the flesh on the thigh is pierced with a fine skewer the juice should be colourless rather than pink.

Meanwhile, fry the bacon and mushrooms in 1 dessertspoon of the remaining butter and when they are cooked add the lemon juice. Serve the chicken on a hot dish with the bacon and mushroom dressing poured over. Garnish with watercress and crisps.

serves 4

Devonshire Michaelmas Goose

I am very fond of the human touch with which many of the old methods end—and this is the one I like best.

To roast a fat goose from the stubble: Stuff the body of the bird well with sage and onion, then tie the ends of the legs together. Cover the bird with fat and roast slowly at 150-170°C (300-325°F, Gas Mark 2-3), allowing 12 minutes per 450g (1 lb.). After half the cooking time, baste well, then dredge over the whole body of the goose with seasoned flour. Put back into the oven, basting again at half-hourly intervals and then dredging.

When the bird is done, pour the fat out of the tin except for a spoonful, stir in a little flour and then 275 ml (half a pint) of good stock made from the giblets and salt and pepper to taste. Boil this up, letting it thicken well. Serve the goose with this gravy, apple sauce and creamed potatoes.

'Some like the crust formed by the flour dredged over the bird to eat, but if not liked it can be broken off and fed to the dogs.'

Roast Turkey

The best method is to cook the bird slowly, breast side down to start with, and then it bastes itself. If the back is thoroughly covered with either cooking foil or bacon fat, the bird should only need to be looked at once or twice during the cooking and it should be turned breast upwards about half an hour before the end of the required time.

Timing: allow 30 minutes for the first 450 g (1 lb.), 15 minutes per 450g (1 lb.) for the remainder, starting at 230°C (450°F, Gas mark 8) for the first hour and then reducing the heat to 180°C (350°F, Gas Mark 4) for the rest of the time.

With this method it may be best to wrap the legs with a double layer of cooking foil which is removed towards the end of the cooking just to allow the skin to brown. This will prevent the flesh on the legs from becoming overcooked or tough.

The stuffing can be the traditional sausage meat or, more exotically, chestnut stuffing for the inside and sausage meat or parsley, thyme and lemon for the breast. But my family like piles of crisp brown sausages done in the pan with the bird and extra stuffing, crisp as well, done in a separate pan.

To help flavour the breast you can tie a faggot of herbs under the foil, lying along the curve of each wing bone, adding some slivers of fat bacon at the same time. What a pity that all our cookery books seem to have decided that bouquet garni is somehow more high class than the old 'faggot of herbs' which I like so much better. You will find a method for making this under the herbs in the vegetable section (p. 85).

EGGS

Bacon and Egg Pie

There are many variations of this old West Country dish but I have chosen only two. The original recipe is too rich and solid for most modern tastes; it calls for a plate to be lined with shortcrust pastry, this is then lined with bacon rashers and eggs are broken into it, more bacon on top and a pastry crust on top of this!

Bacon Custard Pie

225g (½ lb.) shortcrust pastry
100g (¼ lb.) chopped ham
1 tablespoon chopped parsley
salt
black pepper
4 eggs, beaten

Line an 18-cm (7-inch) shallow dish with half the pastry and cover with ham. Sprinkle over the parsley, salt and pepper. Pour on the eggs, cover with the remaining pastry and bake in a hot oven, 200°C (400°F, Gas Mark 6), for about 30 minutes until golden brown.

serves 4

Bacon and Egg Cake

4 rashers bacon
1 dessertspoon cornflour
150ml (¼ pint) milk
4 eggs
salt
black pepper
1 dessertspoon butter
1 dessertspoon chopped chives
   or parsley

Remove the rind from the bacon, fry or grill it and keep hot.

Meanwhile, slake the cornflour with a little milk and mix with the beaten eggs. Whisk in the remaining milk until the mixture is smooth, and season to taste.

Melt the butter in an omelette pan and when it is hot pour in the egg mixture. Cook quickly until nearly set, drawing the cooked mixture from the sides to the centre with a palette knife. Arrange the bacon on top, then put the pan under a hot grill for a few minutes until the surface of the cake browns and sets. Slide onto a hot dish, sprinkle with the chives or parsley and serve at once.

serves 4

Egg and Cheese Cakes

4 eggs, beaten
1 tablespoon grated onion
⅓ cup flour
⅓ cup cheese
½ teaspoon salt
good pinch black pepper
⅓ cup fat for frying

Mix the eggs with the onion, flour, cheese and seasoning. Heat the fat in a large frying pan until a drop of water sizzles on contact, then drop a large spoonful of the mixture into the fat. Fry the cake until well browned on each side, turning once. Repeat until all the mixture is used up.

Serve promptly with marmalade or jelly.

serves 2

Egg and Potato Pie

6 eggs
675g (1½ lb.) potatoes
100g (¼ lb.) Cheddar cheese, grated
white sauce made with 275ml (½ pint) milk
1 heaped tablespoon chopped parsley

Hard-boil the eggs and then stand them in cold water to avoid dark rings around the yolks. When cold, shell them and slice them.

Peel and parboil the potatoes and slice them ½ – cm (¼ – inch) thick. Use half the potatoes to line the bottom and sides of a 22-cm (8½-inch) greased pie dish and cover with the eggs, reserving some slices for garnish. Sprinkle with the cheese, pour on the sauce into which the parsley has been stirred, cover with the remaining potato slices and then brush over with a little milk.

Bake at 180°C (350°F, Gas Mark 4) until the potatoes are cooked and nicely browned. Garnish with the remaining egg.

serves 3 – 4

Shrimpy Eggs

2-3 dozen shrimps
cayenne pepper
50g (2 oz) butter
3 or 4 eggs
salt
black pepper
hot buttered toast

Shell the shrimps and dust them lightly with cayenne pepper. Melt half the butter in an ovenproof dish in a warm oven, then add the shrimps and heat them for about 15 minutes until warmed through.

Meanwhile, melt the remaining butter over moderate heat, break in the eggs, season and stir for 2 minutes. Add the warmed shrimps, remove the pan from the heat and stir until the mixture is well thickened.

Serve at once with hot toast.

serves 4

Tasty Batter

batter
225g (½ lb.) plain flour
1 teaspoon salt
1 tablespoon margarine, melted
2 eggs
just under 575 ml (1 pint) milk

filling
3 dessertspoons margarine
1 small onion, chopped
1 dessertspoon flour
225g (½ lb.) minced meat
2 tablespoons water
salt
black pepper
1 tablespoon dripping

To make the batter sift the flour and salt into a bowl and make a hollow in the centre of the flour. Add the melted margarine, eggs and a little milk, gradually drawing the flour in from the edges to make a smooth paste. When the mixture is smooth, gradually add the rest of the milk, beating all the time. Cover the bowl and leave it to stand in a cool place for about an hour before using.

To prepare the filling—melt the margarine in a pan, add the onion and fry gently, stirring occasionally, until tender. Stir in the flour, then add the minced meat, water and seasoning. Cook gently for 10 minutes.

Melt the dripping in a fireproof dish and when it is hot pour in enough batter to make a thin layer over the base. Sprinkle with 2 tablespoons or so of meat mixture to make another layer and continue with alternate layers of batter and meat, ending with batter.

Bake in a hot oven 200°C (400°F, Gas Mark 6), for about 1¼ hours. Serve hot.

serves 6

Butter, Cream and Cheese

Butter, Cream and Cheese

Cornish cream, Devonshire butter, Somerset cheese, Dorset honey . . . the land of cream and honey . . . the sleepy, sun-drenched south-west—it sounds like a travel brochure, and certainly hordes of holiday-makers pour down into this area every summer, hoping to find the land of pleasure and plenty. I always hope that they will not be disappointed because, to put it at its very lowest, they bring much-needed cash to our sometimes strained and slow-moving economy. Tourism is so vital a part of that economy that I am sure we must somehow learn to live with it and, indeed, welcome it.

I feel rather ashamed when I hear residents complain of the influx of visitors, and I feel even more ashamed when visitors tell stories of being fleeced by landladies, shop-keepers, hoteliers and licensees. Perhaps, though, it's the sort of love/hate relationship which sometimes has to be between two sets of people.

Be that as it may, the cream, butter, cheese and honey of the south-west have always been famous, and still are, even if some of us feel that there has been over-exposure of some of the more evocative names, usually by the large producers. Today such phrases as 'farmhouse fresh', 'farmer's wife', 'home-baked' and 'country-made' are usually employed to describe something which is a long way from those original qualities. And I am afraid that some of our lovely West Country products will feel the effects of the latest edict against eating too much animal fat such as butter, cream and fatty meat. *I* have lived too long to change and I shall go on eating farmhouse butter and clotted cream, and if I die of a heart attack it will have been worth it!

Somerset has always been noted for its cheese, whose quality stems from the nature of the countryside—the lush water-meadows, luxuriant marsh grazing and the mild air of the Bristol Channel, all of which lent themselves to the particular Somerset type of dairy farming; that is, milk from spring-calving cattle. The traditional Somerset dairy farm was situated in one of the lovely stone-built villages, each farm having extensive grazing on the marshes or water-meadows, as well as its few acres near the farmhouse.

The cows were rough-housed during the winter months, they calved in the spring and were then turned out onto the outlying pastures, never coming in again until the winter weather started. Much of this grazing could be some way from the farm, and it was the custom for the farmer, usually with his wife, to make his way, often in a rather dilapidated pony trap, to where the cattle were, taking with him buckets, stools and the necessary churns. The herd would gather obediently, and down the farmer and his wife would sit to milk. Even ten years ago it was possible to see from the Bristol-Taunton railway or the Wells to Glastonbury road a little huddle of cows clustered round a stooping figure milking into a bucket.

Most of the farmers now use milking 'bails', the bail really being just a mobile milking shed which can be towed by tractor into the field and which provides a little shelter for cow and cowman. It also houses a small motor so that a milking-machine can be used.

But the connection between this kind of dairying and the making of Cheddar cheese may not be immediately obvious. The explanation is that the spring flush of milk came in so strongly that the yields were far more than could be sold on the liquid milk market alone, so cheese-making developed, and each stone farmhouse became its own cheese factory. From this, the reputation of Cheddar cheese was born.

Now, of course, we have cheese-making factories in Cornwall, Devon, Somerset and Dorset, and very good cheese they make, but real farmhouse cheese—the sort that takes the skin off your tongue—can still be bought if you know where to look. Or, if that is too rigorous for you, look for a 'mild' variety on some of the stalls which can be found still in West Country markets. The day of the enormous 60 lb. linen-wrapped cheese from which a generous wedge would be cut is nearly gone, I'm afraid; the shop-keepers don't like them (there is too much waste, and you need a cheese-board and cutter to cut them—and also some skill), so instead we get those pre-wrapped oblongs. I suppose we must be glad there is still good cheese in the packs at all and that it hasn't all gone into little foil-wrapped pieces in boxes, which to me isn't cheese at all.

There were other local cheeses besides Cheddar, of course: Dorset Blue Vinney, now alas unobtainable since the last farmhouse cheese-maker decided it no longer paid to produce the smooth, creamy, delectable 'blue' cheese which took its name from the veins of colour running through it. and Tiverton cheese? – perhaps the less said about that the better. It was made, we are told, by one local history book, 'of skimmed milk and was so hard that even the dogs barked at it'.

There is no better meal in the world than Dorset Knobs—small, crisp, round, hard-baked rolls—with farmhouse butter and a wedge of farmhouse cheese. And if you are one of those who say butter should not be eaten with cheese, may I recall the old saying about butter: 'Bad cheese needs it, good cheese deserves it.'

As with cheeses, from similar economic necessity the people of Devon and Cornwall made clotted cream. Small isolated farms, with a cow or two producing milk in the days long before the great milk lorries wound their way up and down the narrow lanes or over the long lonely stretches of moor, had to find a market for their product which would not keep. So the milk was left to stand in shallow bowls, then the contents heated gradually—over a wood fire in Devon, more probably a peat one in Cornwall—then cooled until the lovely wrinkled top had formed, when it was lifted off into a shallow bowl and so taken to market. Perhaps a tenth of the bulk of the original milk could be sold this way for a good price and the skim kept for the calves.

The difference between Devon and Cornish creams? It is a subject no one agrees on. My own theory has always been that Cornish cream was whiter—originally that is—because the pastures were poorer, while Devonshire cream was thick and yellow because the grass was lusher.It is still true today, of course, that the milk from different breeds of cows will produce varying types of cream, but as the 'national herd' is now largely Friesian, the old theories no longer apply and unless you know where to buy it, clotted cream now comes pre-packed in sealed cartons. I'm not entirely sure if this is progress.

No tea in the world quite comes up to a real 'cream tea', preferably prepared on a farm where they make their own cream and serve it to you in a glass bowl with chudleys, cut rounds, tuff cakes or splits, and to top it, strawberry jam in which you find whole berries. This real clotted cream never needs any attention such as whipping or piping; its only decoration is the wrinkled top which, curd-like, conceals the creamier part beneath.

How to keep cheese

Cheese stored for too long in the wrong conditions will become either too dry, mouldy, greasy or even 'crawly'. The best way to keep most average-sized cuts of cheese is to wrap it lightly in a polythene bag and keep it in a cool larder or refrigerator (though not in the ice-box). Under these conditions it should last for at least a week. Grated cheese can be kept in a covered jar in a dry, cool place for several weeks, but it must be dry cheese, otherwise it will grow mouldy. Cheese is easily dried out for storage if it is grated and then left spread out on a large plate in a dry, airy larder for a few hours.

Cheese can safely be bought in as large quantities as the traditional 'truckle' (for Cheddar this is usually 8-12 lb., although it can be even larger) but you should try and obtain one that has already been matured at least to eating stage in the cheese-maker's own storage as you cannot do this at home. Try to buy a cheese which has been bandaged in the traditional way with 'cheese grey'; you can then peel off enough of the cloth to cut out the first wedge, then press the cloth to the surface of the cheese again as closely as you can as this will exclude air and prevent moulding. Store the whole cheese in a cool, dry, airy place, inspect regularly for mould and scrape with a knife if it appears.

BUTTER

Almond Shortbread

100 g + 1 dessertspoon (¼ lb.) butter
150 g + 3 dessertspoons (6 oz) flour
50 g + ½ dessertspoon (2 oz) caster sugar
¼ teaspoon salt
75 g + 1 dessertspoon (3 oz) ground almonds

Beat the butter with a wooden spoon until it is soft (in cold weather the butter may be slightly warmed, but on no account should it be allowed to become oily). Sift the flour, sugar and salt, add the ground almonds and rub the butter into these ingredients, working with the hands until the mixture is pliable.

Butter a 20-cm (8-inch) sandwich tin or a shallow oblong tin. Turn the shortbread mixture into the tin and knead it out to the edges with the knuckles until it is even and flat. Prick all over with a fork and bake in a moderate oven, 180°C (350°F, Gas Mark 4), for about 45 minutes, or until the shortbread is pale brown and firm to the touch.

Leave in the tin and while it is still warm, cut into even pieces. Do not remove the shortbread from the tin until it is nearly cold or it will crumble.*

Shortbread

125 g + 2 dessertspoons (5 oz) flour
25 g (1 oz) rice flour
50 g + ½ dessertspoon (2 oz) caster sugar
100 g + 1 dessertspoon (¼ lb.) butter

Sieve the flours and sugar into a bowl and knead the butter into the dry ingredients by hand. When the mixture binds together, either pack it into a 15-cm (6-inch) baking tin lined with a piece of buttered greaseproof paper, or, turn it onto a lightly floured board and press into a round cake first. Prick a design on top with a fork and crimp the edges using the finger and thumb.

Bake in a moderate oven, 180°C (350°F, Gas Mark 4), for about an hour until firm and lightly browned. Lift carefully from the tin onto a wire tray and dredge with caster sugar. When cold, cut in triangles or fingers.*

* For Plain Shortbread and Rich Shortbread see page 121.

Ginger Shortbread

150 g + 3 dessertspoons (6 oz) flour
50 g + ½ dessertspoon (2 oz) caster sugar
½ – 1 teaspoon ground ginger
100 g + 1 dessertspoon (¼ lb.) butter
25 g (1 oz) chopped crystallized ginger

Sieve the flour, sugar and ground ginger into a bowl and rub in the butter until the mixture resembles breadcrumbs. Add the chopped ginger and knead the mixture until it is smooth. Pack evenly into a 20-cm (8-inch) sandwich tin and crimp the edges between thumb and finger. Prick with a fork and mark triangles on the surface with a sharp knife.

Bake in a moderate oven 180°C (350°F, Gas Mark 4), for about an hour until golden and firm. Do not remove from the tin until cool.

Flavoured Butters

To 50g (2 oz) softened butter add the following ingredients and mix in well (chill slightly before use);

Cod's Roe Butter 50g (2 oz) canned cod's roe, a little lemon juice, salt and pepper.

Watercress Butter 1 tablespoon finely chopped watercress, a little lemon juice, a pinch of salt.

Lemon Butter grated rind of half a lemon, a teaspoon of lemon juice, 1 level dessertspoon caster sugar.

Cheese Butter 40g (1½ oz) finely grated Cheddar cheese, a pinch of dry mustard.

Mint Butter 1 tablespoon finely chopped mint, ½ teaspoon lemon juice, salt and pepper.

Chive Butter 1 dessertspoon finely chopped chives, a pinch of salt.

These quantities are sufficient for four open sandwiches, or to use as accompaniments to fish, meat or vegetable dishes.

CREAM

Almost anything is better with cream has always been my belief, but here are some recipes which can *only* be made with cream.

Burnt Cream

Using equal quantities of baked custard and clotted cream, put a layer of custard in the bottom of a 575ml (1 pint) pie dish, then a layer of clotted cream, continuing with the layers until the dish is full, finishing with a cream layer. Slice some citron very thin and put it on top. Sprinkle with caster sugar and lightly brown under a hot grill.

Allow 100 g (¼ lb.) each of cream and custard for 4 servings for a family meal, but 225 g (½ lb.) of cream to 100 g (¼ lb.) custard makes very rich helpings for a special occasion.

Damask Cream

'Cook cream gently with some mace and cracked cinnamon till delicately flavoured. Add sugar and rosewater, and set it with fine rennet. When cold flood over it soft cream flavoured with rosewater and lightly strewn with powdered sugar. Serve surrounded by deep damask rose petals.'[1]

This recipe is so nearly a poem by itself that I include it just because of that. Rosewater is available from chemists, and deep damask rose petals are hard to find, but for those who are adventurous enough to try, allow 2 tablespoons of rennet to set 575ml (1 pint) of cream.

Syllabub

The syllabub was made according to various recipes in all country districts. It was sometimes served as a drink or it could be an accompaniment to fruit or the base of a trifle. When served as a sweet it was put into syllabub glasses, and at Bath an extra charge was made if it was eaten out of doors because so many glasses got broken.

[1]H.W. Lewer (ed.)

'To make a Silliebube'

(from a farmhouse recipe book dated 1757)

575 ml (1 pint) white wine
575 ml (1 pint) morning's cream
100 g (¼ lb.) sugar

'Put the ingredients in a basin and beat them well together till it come to a froth, then pour it into a Syllabub pot and milk a sufficient quantity of milk into it and let it stand in a cool place till night, for the longer it stand so it grow not sour, the clearer the drink will be and the firmer the curd.'

Solid Syllabub

(a modern method)

2 tablespoons orange juice
2 tablespoons lemon juice
75 g (3 oz) caster sugar
275 ml (½ pint) whipping
cream
1 glass of sherry or 2 glasses
white wine

Combine the fruit juices and sugar, add the cream and wine and whip until very stiff. Turn into individual dishes and chill.

serves 4

Ganache

575 ml (1 pint) of real dairy
cream
1 kg (2 lb.) chocolate
couverture (plain or milk)

A recipe we, in the West Country, have borrowed from Normandy. Ganache, which is a mixture of real dairy cream and chocolate couverture, can be used for filling or topping. It is a delicious and deservedly popular dish and is also useful because it keeps for about three weeks.

Put the chocolate in a bowl and melt over a pan of hot water (but not over direct heat). The temperature of the chocolate should not exceed 46°C (115°F).

Put the cream in a pan, bring it to the boil and pour it over the chocolate, stirring well together immediately. The mixture should be left in a cool place for two days before using.

To use ganache: put it in the bowl of a mixing machine and warm slightly. Then operate the beater arm at the second speed until the mixture becomes a light mass suitable for piping or spreading.

Varieties of ganache can be flavoured with rum, kirsch, coffee, etc., but make it with milk chocolate as the flavour of plain would be too dominant.

Devon Cakes

225 g (½ lb.) clotted cream
450 g (1 lb.) flour
1 egg
225 g (½ lb.) sugar
milk to mix

Rub the cream into the sifted flour, beat in the egg, add the sugar and mix into a smooth paste, adding a little milk if necessary to make the consistency of dough.

Roll out rather thin and cut into small shapes. Sprinkle with granulated sugar, put on a baking tray and bake in a hot oven, 230°C (450°F, Gas Mark 8), for about 10 minutes.

Serve hot with jam or cold with jam and cream.

serves 6

CHEESE

Cheese Eggs

175g (6 oz) Cheddar cheese, grated
6 dessertspoons flour
½ teaspoon Worcester sauce
1 teaspoon salt
pinch cayenne pepper
1 egg, beaten
1-2 tablespoons milk
4 hard-boiled eggs
dry breadcrumbs for coating
deep fat for frying

Mix the cheese, flour, Worcester sauce and seasonings and add the egg and enough milk to bind the ingredients. Mix well.

Using wet hands, coat the eggs completely with the mixture, then roll in the breadcrumbs to coat evenly. Fry in hot, deep fat until golden brown. Drain well and serve hot or cold.

serves 4

Cheese and Onion Pie

pastry
225g (½ lb.) flour
pinch of salt
pinch of cayenne pepper
pinch of baking powder
75g + ½ dessertspoon (3 oz) margarine
100g + 1 dessertspoon (¼ lb.) Cheddar cheese, finely grated
cold water to bind

Prepare the pastry, then divide it in two and roll out each half to fit a 23-cm (9-inch) pie plate, Line the plate with one half of the pastry and prick with a fork.

Slice the onions and cook them gently in butter, then put alternate layers of cheese and onion on the pastry base, seasoning each layer and beginning and ending with cheese. Cover with the remaining pastry.

Bake in a moderately hot oven, 200°C (400°F, Gas Mark 6) for 30-35 minutes. Serve hot or cold.

serves 6

filling
4 large onions
25-50g (1-2 oz) butter
175g (6 oz) Cheddar cheese,
  grated

½ level teaspoon grated
  nutmeg
1 level teaspoon salt
pinch of pepper
2 teaspoons Worcester sauce

Cheesy Fruit Pie

350g (¾ lb.) shortcrust pastry
1 dessertspoon butter
2 dessertspoons plain flour
150ml (¼ pint) milk
pepper
salt
100g (¼ lb.) Cheddar cheese,
  grated
1 egg, beaten
175g (6 oz) sultanas

Divide the pastry in two and roll out each half to fit an 20-cm (8-inch) pie plate. Line the plate with one half.

Make a rich cheese sauce with the butter, flour, milk, seasoning and 75g (3 oz) of the cheese. Draw the pan off the heat, add the egg, stir and leave to cool.

Put alternate layers of sultanas and cheese filling on the pastry base and cover with the remaining pastry. Finish the edges neatly and snip the top crust in several places with a pair of scissors. Brush with beaten egg or milk and sprinkle with the remaining cheese.

Bake in a fairly hot oven, 200°C (400°F, Gas Mark 6) for 30 – 40 minutes. Serve hot or cold.

serves 4

Cheesy Potato Cakes

450g (1 lb.) potatoes, peeled
  and finely grated
225g (½ lb.) Cheddar cheese,
  grated
50g (2 oz) self-raising flour
½ level teaspoon salt
fat for frying

Mix together the potatoes, cheese, flour and salt. Heat fat, to a depth of about 1cm (½ inch), in a frying pan and fry tablespoons of the mixture on both sides until golden-brown. Drain well and serve hot.

serves 3 – 4

Cheese Bake

100g (¼ lb.) day-old bread ,
  crusts removed
575ml (1 pint) milk
½ teaspoon salt
pinch cayenne pepper
1 teaspoon made mustard
2 eggs, beaten
175g (6 oz) Cheddar cheese,
  grated

Crumble the bread roughly into a bowl. Bring the milk to the boil, pour it over the crumbs and leave to soak for 30 minutes. Mash well with a fork to break up the soaked crumbs. Add the seasonings, eggs and cheese and mix well.

Pour into a 20-cm (8-inch) greased pie-dish and bake in a moderate oven, 160°C (325°F, Gas Mark 3), for about 45 minutes until well-risen and just set. Serve at once.

serves 4

Somerset Savoury

4 slices thickly-cut stale bread, well-buttered
175g (6 oz) Cheddar cheese, thinly sliced
225g (½ lb.) onions, thinly sliced
salt
pepper
1 cupful top of milk

Line a 20-cm (8-inch) fireproof dish with the slices of bread. Add a layer of cheese, onions and seasoning, then another layer of bread followed by cheese and onions again. Continue until the ingredients are used up, seasoning each layer and ending with bread.

Dot over the top with butter and bake in a hot oven, 220°C (425°F, Gas Mark 7), for about 35 minutes until the bread is brown and the onion cooked. Remove from the oven, pour over the milk and serve at once.

serves 4

Cheese Fingers

6 tablespoons milk
1 egg, beaten
4 level tablespoons Cheddar cheese, finely grated
2 slices of bread cut in ½-cm (¼-inch, thick fingers)
butter for frying

Mix together the milk, egg and cheese and stand the bread fingers in this until they are thoroughly soaked.

Heat a little butter to a pale golden-brown in a small frying pan and fry the bread on both sides until lightly browned. Serve hot.

serves 2

Meat and Game

Meat

The West Country has never been a rich region; we have too few cities with too many miles between them, and although the land has rich pasture areas, some parts—Dartmoor, Exmoor, Bodmin Moor, the Somerset Levels—have always been and always will be unproductive. Meat was therefore a luxury, even—in fact mostly—for those who produced it. Farmers who fattened beef sent it to market to sell and themselves ate Cornish pasties or, I'm afraid, New Zealand lamb. This has left its mark on West Country regional recipes for meat cookery. They tend to be for ways of using the cheap cuts bulked out, not, as in Norfolk, with dumplings or in Yorkshire with Yorkshire pudding, but by stews 'extended' with various vegetables.

Traditional meat cookery was also governed by the very late introduction into the area of roasting ovens. Cooking was done until the turn of this century, or even later, on the open fire and the traditional oven built into the side of the open hearth was used only for bread or cakes. And although the turning spit was occasionally used, far more faith was placed in the 'baking oven' or 'baking pan'.

When the spit was used with peat or wood-burning fires it would have been set horizontally on spit stands, the width of the fire being great enough to allow this; when coal fires became usual, the spit hung vertically from a hook or beam. For the horizontal method the meat, fish or poultry to be cooked was threaded onto the sharp end of the spit and a dripping pan put underneath. It was then the task of the cook or whoever happened to be about to turn the spit round regularly and see that the food cooked evenly. A surprising number of quite different foods could be cooked in this way and a medieval recipe I found tells the cook to 'thread dates and figs, apples and oddments onto the spit, then as they roast baste them with a good batter, till all is embedded in a thick crisp crust, when the batter is all used, strew sugar and spice over and continue turning until the whole is firm and brown'. Perhaps worth trying on a barbecue?

In addition to the spit, foods would be baked in what in Devon was called a bacon boiler in which, like the modern pressure cooker, a variety of foods for the same meal could be cooked. But I don't mean that everything was *boiled*; earthenware jars packed with poultry were sunk into the liquid, puddings wrapped in cloth were hung to boil, meat could be pot-roasted by putting it into an earthenware container with a few vegetables at the bottom and a close-fitting lid on top. The variations were endless. I have just such a bacon boiler in my possession, cracked, alas, so that we can no longer use it for our bacon but, as with so many old kitchen utensils, I find it makes a beautiful plant container.

The peat fires of the far south-west can still be found today in remote areas, though peat has now become something to put on your garden rather than a sweet-smelling, slow-burning fire. The use of peat is said to have been the reason for the characteristic smoky taste of the Cornish clotted cream, and the Cornish pasty was ideal for baking in a pot oven in the slow heat of the peat ash. But it was not possible to roast on a peat fire and I suspect this is why so few Devon and Cornish recipes called for roasted meat, while in the richer counties of Somerset or Dorset, wood was more easily obtainable, and near the Somerset coal mines coal would have been cheap. But to burn coal on an open hearth with little or no draught was asking for trouble and it was only when chimneys became more common that coal was widely used. (It is interesting to notice that in many of the old agricultural books coal is referred to as 'sea coal' because that is how it was transported but in Somerset, alone of our south-western counties, it is always called just coal; to the inhabitants of districts round Radstock it was a familiar commodity.)

Regretfully, I have never been able to find one of the baking ovens, but it has been described to me as a large cast-iron pan, probably of at least two gallons' capacity, with a close-fitting lid and one or more handles. The meat was put into the pan with a good lump of dripping, the lid fitted on closely and the pan then put into the hottest part of the huge open fire. Hot ashes were raked up over the sides and top of the pan, and the meat roasted without further attention. Basting would not have been necessary as steam from the meat would rise to the lid of the pan and then fall back, together with fat globules, onto the joint.

Looking back now, I can see that the cottagers of my childhood in a remote Cotswold village were all in the position of having no oven, because I can still see the village children flying down the street on a Sunday morning, each with a pan close-covered with a cloth from which issued the most appetizing smells—the family joint cooked by an obliging baker in his bread oven. It didn't seem in the least strange to me at the time; I merely thought it was an infinitely more exciting way of having the Sunday dinner cooked than my mother just putting the dish into our vast old coal-fired range.

When we first came to Devon 30 years ago, a delightful old farmer's wife, herself then 82, described to me in the minutest detail the preparation needed to provide, with only the baking oven, a good three-course meal for ten or a dozen hungry men. When I asked if it were not very hard work she said, 'Yes, but of course there were always two or three girls; the dairy maid, the poultry maid and the inside girl, and one or two of the family were usually here as well.'

So today, having no dairy maids and usually daughters who go out to work themselves, the West Countrywoman, along with all other country housewives, has to turn to convenience foods, and with meat this usually means ready-prepared dishes in tins or packets or, increasingly, freezer packs. Our local butchers have responded to this demand with great vigour and in almost every small town and some villages you can find a butcher who will sell you a whole lamb or a quarter of beef, and who will cut and wrap it as well; not to mention the village shop which carries in its freezer small packs of meat suitable for the person living alone or wanting something tasty for 'fayther's tea'.

So many women work today, whether full or part-time, and this fact, together with the almost total disappearance of the local bus service in rural areas, has meant that in most cases the car has to be got out perhaps once a week; so obviously one buys as much as possible during the shopping expedition. Certainly the small butchers' stalls seem to have disappeared almost completely from the local markets, so that what I find the most interesting development of the freezer market is the farmer/producer who sells meat at the farm gate.

These outlets are, of course, rigorously controlled by public health regulations, but there are other problems—for instance, certain authorities are becoming increasingly concerned by the question of access into sometimes dangerous farmyards and along narrow, winding lanes. And local passions and rivalries sometimes become enraged when the small butcher sees his trade being taken away by a farmer whose buildings are de-rated and who in any case sometimes does not carry the very heavy overheads he has to pay. However, my chief concern is that the farm gate sales often provide a second income for the small farmer who has seen his sales of eggs and poultry being taken over by the big specialist producers and whose only other outlet for his livestock is the local auction market.

I said previously that beef and lamb were not the basis of many truly regional dishes, but with pork and bacon it is an enitrely different matter. Climatically and economically the south-west has always been the home of the cottager's pig, of which Cobbett writes in his *Cottage Economy* of 1821:

> Make him quite fat by all means. If he can walk two hundred yards at a time he is not well fatted. Lean bacon is the most wasteful thing a family can have. The man who cannot live on solid fat bacon, well fed and well cured, wants the sweet sauce of labour or is fit for the hospital.

Although I doubt if any modern pig-keeper would agree with the description of the state the pig should be in before killing, as described by a cottage-pig-killing friend of mine, 'Her should be so fat her can't get out of the hovel.' The modern housewife would turn pale at the sight of the fat bacon which used to be on sale in the butchers' shops when we first came to Devon, because there really was two-and-a-half to three inches of fat with no lean at all. The countrymen round us would take a fair sized lump of this for the 'levenses' (which, incidentally, they always took at 10 o'clock).

The cottagers' method was to fatten, in a home-built sty, one or two pigs fed mostly on household waste mixed with middlings, a term which covered most tail-end corn, barley, wheat, oats—in fact anything the mill would sell fairly cheaply. Then, when the pig was really fat, some neighbour— probably a butcher—would come in and kill it for you, leaving you, after the necessary formalities, with a quite terrifying mound of pig meat with which to deal. The main joints were easy, but the rest—lights, liver, heart, lungs, kidneys, head, trotters, not to mention the chitterlings and the flead— oh dear!

The meat produced by this haphazard method of feeding would be totally unacceptable today when no one will eat a morsel of fat even if interspersed with lean. I can neither explain nor condemn this modern detestation of fat, and it has made the breeding and feeding of the animals and selling of meat a much more difficult business. But the day of the rather lofty attitude adopted by farmers towards marketing of any sort is past. More and more liaison is going on between the breeders and the butchers and you would have to go a long way to find better beef, lamb or pork than we produce here in the West Country.

Nowadays if you want to kill a pig you ring up the local slaughterhouse, they fetch it and 24 hours later you are told to collect the bits you want. Easier, certainly, but I must confess I felt a sense of enormous achievement when I had reduced that mound of meat to manageable proportions. Lacking a deep freeze (an almost unheard-of item in those days), we had to eat pork day after day; what we didn't eat was salted by one or other of the time-honoured methods, leaving us with delicious bits such as 'scratching' (the mesenteric layer of the intestine after the lard had been melted from it and which made the most gorgeous pastry) and of course the lard itself, not to be compared with modern 'soft spreads' or emulsified fats.

It irks me considerably when I hear people say: 'I always buy Danish bacon, it's so consistent', when our farmers are working hard to breed and feed to rigorous standards, though I agree that in the past there were too many 'elephants' or 'greyhounds' sent off to the bacon factory. It also irks me when people come back from continental holidays drooling over the foods they have seen in the country markets and comment disparagingly on what is avilable in our own shops or market stalls. Some of them must be in a state of bemusement at being in foreign parts because I doubt very much if they would buy the charcuterie and cooked meats they see abroad if they were available here. The market stalls of Brittany and Normandy look entrancing, I know, but our public health authorities would never allow food to be displayed in like manner. Here, everything has to be behind breath-plates, under covers, wrapped or pre-packed, often to the detriment of its looks—though not, of course, to its cleanliness. I appreciate this aspect, but I think we have gone too far.

Game

The West, never having been a district of great estates, game cookery does not figure very largely in the old recipes. I suspect that apart from what one might call the grand recipes for the squire's table, most of the remainder would be more suitable for birds or beasts which had been poached. So in the recipe pages you will find mostly old country recipes for using the humbler species—hares, rabbits, pigeons—all of which probably found their way into the capacious pockets of knowledgeable village poachers.

There is a tip from a cottager-poacher which I particularly like: 'If the squire's pheasants were invading your garden to eat the peas, you smeared a paper bag inside with treacle, put a few raisins inside—to which pheasants are very partial—and put the bag down alongside the rows of peas. The bird stuck in his head and unable to see his way out stayed there until it was convenient for you to fetch him.'

Hares are difficult to come by today, and even the humble rabbit often comes from China, dismembered and frozen. But nothing is finer than a country rabbit well-cooked and turned into a pie, while the noble hare makes a truly regal dish when jugged with port. Pigeons when cheap can be used plentifully, but they make a poor dish if you have to count the cost. All these species would traditionally have been made into what we would call today a pâté, but which appear in the old country recipes as 'potted' hare or pigeon, because our ancestors did not have the benefit of the modern liquidizer and so slow cooking was necessary.

MEAT

Pot-Roast Beef

joint of topside
1 onion
3 cloves
1 bayleaf
prepared mixed vegetables (see method)
2 tablespoons flour
stock or water for gravy
gravy browning

Wipe the joint and see that it is well tied and firmly secured with a skewer. Put it in a heavy saucepan with a little melted fat to prevent burning. Add the onion stuck with the cloves, and a bayleaf. Cover with a well-fitting lid. Set the pan over a good heat, lowering the heat as soon as the meat begins to sizzle (if you like both sides of the meat browned, turn it at once).

For small joints, allow 15 minutes per 450g (1 lb.) plus a further 15 minutes; for larger joints, 20 minutes per 450g (1 lb.) plus 15 minutes.

An hour before the meat is cooked, add peeled potatoes, carrots, large onions and turnip if liked. Five minutes before serving, lift the joint out onto a hot dish and pile the vegetables round it. Keep hot in the oven while preparing the gravy.

To make the gravy, pour off all but a little fat from the pan. Gradually stir in the flour and let it cook for 2 minutes. Stir in the stock or hot water and allow the gravy to thicken by simmering, stirring often. Darken with browning if necessary and test for seasoning. Pour the gravy over the meat and vegetables and serve at once.

Pressure-cooking method: brown the meat in hot fat in the pressure-cooker without the lid. Add 275ml (½ pint) water, cover tightly and cook for 10 minutes per 450g (1 lb.) at 15 lb. pressure.

Potted Beef

(A Devon farmhouse recipe)

1kg (2 lb.) beef, rather lean
about 225g (½ lb.) good dripping
salt
black pepper
powdered mace

Put the beef into a stone jar with the dripping, cover it very closely and let it bake slowly or else set it in a pan of boiling water for about four hours.

Take the meat out and, whilst still hot, pound it with a pestle and mortar, moistening with the gravy from the jar and adding salt, pepper and mace to taste as you work. It should start dry, but gradually take up all the grease and juice from the pot while being pounded. When quite smooth and soft, put it into the jar which has been rubbed with a clove of garlic or onion.

serves 6

Rolled Steak and Puffs

(A Dorset recipe)

1kg (2 lb.) good steak, cut in
    one piece about 2-cm
    (¾-inch) thick

seasoned filling
1 teaspoon dripping
1 cup fine breadcrumbs
good pinch mixed herbs
black pepper
salt
1 small onion, finely minced

batter for puffs
1 egg
275ml (½ pint) milk
100g (¼ lb.) flour
pinch of salt

flour to dust
pinch of sugar
dripping to roast

Make the filling by rubbing the dripping into the breadcrumbs and then mixing in the herbs and seasoning. Spread this over the steak, roll it up and secure with a skewer. Dust a little flour and a pinch of sugar over the roll (the sugar imparts a delicious flavour and makes a nice brown gravy), place in a greased roasting pan and dot dripping over the top. Roast at 200°C (400°F, Gas Mark 6) for about 1½ hours, basting frequently.

Meanwhile, prepare the batter: beat the egg thoroughly, mix in the milk and sift in the flour and salt. About 20 minutes before the meat is cooked, add the batter to the roasting pan, 1 dessertspoon at a time, keeping each spoonful separate.

Serve the steak on a hot dish with the Dorset Puffs, accompanied by brown gravy and vegetables.

serves 6

Cornish Pasty (Traditional)

450g (1 lb.) steak
450g (1 lb.) potatoes
100g (¼ lb.) swede
450g (1 lb.) good shortcrust
    pastry

This is the recipe for the traditional Cornish pasty which, in good times, when there was plenty of meat, was a splendid meal—the men could take it to work and the women folk knew they had been properly fed. And in bad times it could still be quite filling, although the mixture might be more vegetables than meat. I think it could be called the first take-away convenience food ever known. It was always eaten in the hand, straight from the pastry, and was never cut with knife and fork.

Cut the meat, potatoes and swede into dice and mix well together (seasoning can be added but this was not usual and no liquid need be added because this will come from the uncooked meat and vegetables).

Roll out the pastry and cut in four pieces each about the size of a tea plate. Put a quarter of the filling on one side of one piece of pastry, brush round the edges with beaten egg and fold the pastry over. Then set the pasty on its base, crimping by hand and getting a good firm closure. Make up the remaining pastry and filling into three more pasties and cook in a moderate oven, 180°C (350°F, Gas Mark 4), for at least an hour.

serves 4

Cornish Pasty (Modern)

225g (½ lb.) minced beef
50g (2 oz) potato, diced
50g (2 oz) swede, diced
50g (2 oz) onion, chopped
seasoning
stock or water to moisten
450g (1 lb.) shortcrust pastry

Proceed as for the traditional method but moisten the ingredients as you mix them, as the minced beef will not produce any liquor. Cook at 200°C (400°F, Gas Mark 6) for about 25 minutes.

An even quicker way is to cook all the fillings first, but this doesn't really pass muster and I refuse to call it a pasty at all. I was once offered, at a catering exhibition, a sample of Cornish Pasty essence—I shudder to think what was in it.

serves 2

Pork Dumplings

225g (½ lb.) salt bacon, finely
  chopped
1 large onion, sliced thinly
1 apple, grated or finely
  chopped
3 or 4 sage leaves
1 tablespoon golden syrup or
  honey
225g (½ lb.) pastry crust for
  boiling (made with raw
  bacon fat)

Mix together the bacon, onion, apple, sage and syrup and stuff the pastry crust with this. Seal closely, filling any cracks with water and pushing the edges together again. Boil the dumpling for about 1 hour 20 minutes and serve very hot. It should be full of rich, savoury juice from the chopped onion and fat pork.

makes 8-10

Pot-Roast Belly of Pork

Proceed exactly as for Pot-Roast Beef (p. 56), but use mostly sage for seasoning and more onion than any other vegetable. Some peeled, chopped apples may also be added to the vegetables.

If the joint has much skin, score it well, but do not turn while cooking as this spoils the crackling.

Devonshire Pie

1kg (2 lb.) pork chops
1 kg (2 lb.) tart apples
2 teaspoons sugar
allspice
2 onions, sliced
salt
pepper
150ml (¼ pint) gravy
175g (6 oz) flaky pastry

Trim the chops and cut them short. Peel, core and slice the apples and put a layer in the bottom of a 25-cm (10-inch) pie dish. Sprinkle with sugar and allspice, then add a layer of onion. Season with salt and pepper, then cover with a layer of chops. Repeat the layers, with seasoning, until the ingredients are used up. Pour in the gravy and cover with flaky pastry.

Bake in a hot oven, 230°C (450°F, Gas Mark 8), for about 10 minutes until the pastry is risen, then reduce the heat to 190°C (375°F, Gas Mark 5) and bake for a further 1½ hours (covering the pastry if necessary to prevent over-browning).

serves 6

Bacon Hotpot

175g (6 oz) dried butter beans
450g (1 lb.) piece of streaky
    bacon (or several smaller
    pieces, but *not* thin rashers)
1 large onion
2 stalks celery, trimmed
salt
pepper
water to cover
1 dessertspoon treacle
½ teaspoon made mustard
1 teaspoon brown sugar

Soak the beans overnight and drain them before using. Cut the bacon into large dice and put them in a casserole or heavy saucepan. Add the beans, onion, celery and seasoning and enough water just to cover. Put on a well-fitting lid and cook either in a slow, preheated oven 120°C (250°F, Gas Mark ½), or over a low flame.

After 45 minutes, add a little more liquid if the dish is dry. Then lift out the bacon pieces, arrange the vegetables in a layer on the bottom of the pan and replace the bacon on top of them (this helps the bacon to crisp and no more liquid should be added after this stage).

Cook for a further 45 minutes and add the treacle, mustard and sugar just before serving. Serve straight from the pan.

serves 3-4

Savoury Plait

350g (¾ lb.) shortcrust pastry
350g (¾ lb.) sausage meat
2 tablespoons chopped fresh
    onion (or 1 dessertspoon)
    dried onion
1 egg
2 teaspoons mixed herbs
salt
pepper
beaten egg

Roll the pastry out in a rectangle about 1 cm (½ inch) thick and as near as possible to 25 cm (10 inches) long by 15 cm (6 inches) wide. Cut it neatly to that size.

Mix the sausage meat with the onion, egg, herbs and seasoning, stirring well together. Shape the mixture into a roll about 20 cm (8 inches) long and 6 cm (2 inches) wide and place it in the middle of the pastry so that its length lies along the length of the pastry. Brush over the exposed pastry with beaten egg (this helps it to stick to the meat).

Using a sharp knife, cut 1½ cm (⅝ inch) wide strips of pastry *across* the width, running from the long edge to beside the meat roll (see diagram 1) but leaving the pastry beneath the roll uncut as the base. Plait strips in a criss-cross over the meat (see diagram 2), brushing on more egg as necessary. Finish the ends neatly, cutting off any excess pastry. Brush over the plait with beaten egg and bake in a moderate oven, 200°C (400°F, Gas Mark 6), for about 45 minutes until golden brown.

serves 6

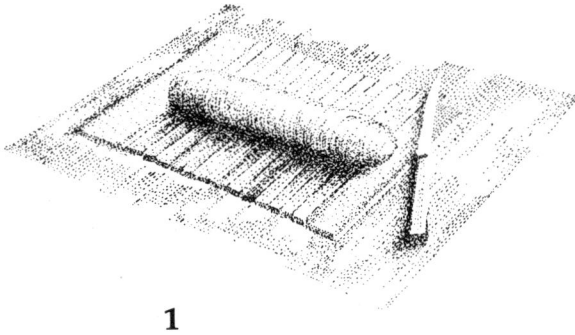

1

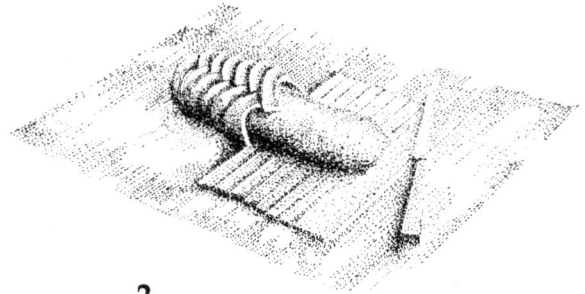

2

Stuffed Roast Breast of Mutton

breast of mutton
salt
pepper

forcemeat
1 cup breadcrumbs
1 dessertspoon chopped
   parsley
good pinch thyme
1 level teaspoon grated lemon
   peel
1 teaspoon chopped mint
salt
pepper
egg or milk to moisten

Lay the meat flat and take out the small bones. Cut it across deeply in several places and season the cuts with salt and pepper.

Make a forcemeat, mixing the dry ingredients first and then moistening with beaten egg or milk. Stuff the cuts in the meat with this and spread the remainder over the meat. Roll up and tie securely. Press the stuffed meat into a square roasting tin or ovenproof dish, dot with a little dripping and cover with greaseproof paper.

Cook in a hot oven, 230°C (450°F, Gas Mark 8), for 2 hours, removing the paper about 15 minutes before the meat is ready to allow it to brown. Slice vertically to carve and serve hot or cold.

Lamb Mould

1 tablespoon gelatine
275ml (½ pint) hot water
1 teaspoon lemon juice
2 dessertspoons caster sugar
1 teaspoon salt
5 dessertspoons vinegar
450g (1 lb.) cooked lamb, diced
    fine
1¼ cupfuls finely shredded
    cabbage
1 tablespoon cooked peas
1 hard-boiled egg, sliced

Dissolve the gelatine in the hot water and add the lemon juice, sugar, salt and vinegar. Strain and set aside to cool.

As soon as the gelatine mixture begins to set, add the lamb, cabbage, peas and eff,egg, mixing gently. Turn into a 725-ml (1½-pint) wet mould and leave in a cool place until set.

Serve turned out on a bed of lettuce leaves accompanied by mayonnaise and tomatoes.

serves 4

Somerset Liver Roll

675g (1½ lb.) liver
1 onion, sliced
fat for frying
2 dessertspoons flour
150ml (¼ pint) milk
100g (¼ lb.) mashed potato
salt
pepper

Slice the liver, fry it with the onion, remove both from the pan and then chop the liver.

Make a gravy, using the fat in the pan, with the flour and milk. Return the liver and onion to the pan and mix in the potato and seasoning. Shape the mixture into a roll, using floured hands, and put it in a roasting tin in which a little dripping has been melted. Bake in a moderate oven, 190°C (375°F, Gas Mark 5), for 45 minutes.

serves 4

GAME

Poacher's Rabbit

one 1¾kg (4 lb.) rabbit
seasoned flour
2-3 onions, chopped
100g (¼ lb.) mushrooms,
    chopped
2-3 potatoes, thinly sliced
4 teaspoons tarragon vinegar
generous 275ml (½ pint) stock
4 rashers bacon

Cut the rabbit into serving pieces and soak in salted water overnight. Dry the pieces well and coat with seasoned flour.

In a well-buttered casserole make layers of rabbit, onion and mushroom and finish with a layer of potatoes. Sprinkle over the vinegar and pour on the stock. Finally lay the bacon rashers on top.

Cover and cook in a moderate oven, 190°C (375°F, Gas Mark 5), for about 2 hours, removing the lid about 20 minutes before the end to allow the rashers to brown.

serves 6

Harvest Rabbit

2 small rabbits
dripping
6 prunes, soaked overnight
   and drained
2 bunches fresh herbs
seasoned flour
2 large onions, sliced thinly, or
   several spring onions
2 thin slices fat bacon
stock

forcemeat balls
100g (¼ lb.) chopped bacon
   (or suet)
25g (1 oz) chopped chives (or
young onion tops)
1 tablespoon sweet marjoram
1 tablespoon chopped parsley
100 g (¼ lb.) fresh
   breadcrumbs
salt
pepper
2 eggs

Skin, draw and cut off the heads, scuts and feet of the rabbits. Wash the prepared rabbits well and soak in salt water for 15 minutes. Dry thoroughly, then fry whole in dripping until pale golden brown all over. Drain off any excess fat. Under the ribs of each rabbit stuff 3 prunes and a bunch of herbs. Coat thickly with seasoned flour.

Cover the base of a large, deep ovenproof dish with the onions. Lay the floured rabbits on top with a slice of bacon over each and just cover with stock. Bake slowly, uncovered, at 150°C (300°F, Gas Mark 2), for 2 hours.

Meanwhile, prepare forcemeat balls of the bacon, herbs, breadcrumbs and seasoning bound with the eggs. Fry the balls until they are deep brown outside (they should cut bright green inside, so use plenty of fresh herbs).

Serve the rabbits on a warm dish, garnished with the onions and forcemeat balls. Strain the liquid in which they have been cooked and serve separately as gravy.

serves 4

Somerset Rabbit

675g - 1kg (1½-2 lb.) rabbit
   joints
2 tablespoons seasoned flour
50g (2 oz) dripping or lard
1 teaspoon meat extract
1 tablespoon tomato ketchup
575ml (1 pint) stock
1 onion, peeled and sliced
4 carrots, peeled and sliced
1 turnip, peeled and diced
a pinch of mixed herbs
salt
pepper
275ml (½ pint) cider

Wash and dry the rabbit joints and toss in seasoned flour. Fry lightly in melted fat in a flameproof casserole for a few minutes until just brown. Remove the rabbit from the pan and set aside.

Add any remaining flour to the fat in the pan, stir well and cook for 2 minutes. Stir in the meat extract, tomato ketchup and stock, and continue stirring until smooth. Bring to the boil, then add the onion, carrots, turnip, rabbit joints, herbs and seasoning. Cover, bring back to the boil, then simmer gently for an hour before adding the cider and adjusting seasoning to taste. Cover and simmer for a further 30 minutes or until tender.

Serve with redcurrant jelly.

serves 4

Jugged Hare

1 hare
seasoned flour
a bunch of sweet herbs
   (chervil, thyme, tarragon)
6 allspice
2 onions, each stuck with 3
   cloves
1 level teaspoon salt
½ teaspoon black pepper
2 or 3 strips lemon peel
25g (1 oz) butter
25g (1 oz) flour
2 tablespoons mushroom or
   tomato ketchup
1 wine glass of port

Wash the hare, cut it into small joints and coat each piece in seasoned flour. Put the meat in a heavy pan with the herbs, allspice, onions, salt, pepper and lemon peel. Cover with cold water, bring to simmering point and simmer, covered, for about 2 hours until tender.

Remove the joints of hare from the liquid in the pan and arrange them on a warm serving dish. Keep hot while preparing the gravy.

Melt the butter in a small saucepan, stir in the flour and cook for 2-3 minutes. Mix in the liquid in which the hare was cooked and stir until the gravy thickens. Add the ketchup and port. Pour the gravy over the hare and let it stand where it will keep hot, but not continue cooking, for 10 minutes.

Serve with forcemeat balls and redcurrant jelly.

serves 6

Roast Saddle of Hare

saddle of one large hare
black pepper
4-6 rashers of bacon
dripping
flour
stock or water
½ wineglass port

Dredge the meat well with black pepper, wrap the bacon round it, then wrap in greaseproof paper and put into a covered pan with knobs of dripping (the double wrapping of bacon and paper keeps the meat very moist and the hot dripping in the pan helps draw the bacon fat—no basting is needed).

Roast in a hot oven, 230°C (450°F, Gas Mark 8), for 20-30 minutes. When cooked, unwrap the paper, transfer the hare to a warm dish and keep hot.

Make a roux by adding flour to the fat in the roasting pan. Stir in the stock or water and let it thicken. Meanwhile, carve the meat from the saddle and put it into an ovenware dish. Pour over the gravy into which the port has been stirred. Cover the dish and put back into the hot oven for a further 15 minutes.

serves 2-4

Somerset is one of the few places in England where venison is still quite common—I have seen it in butchers' shops in Dunster and other places near Exmoor.

Venison should be hung for eight to ten days, and as the meat has very little fat it should be well-basted during cooking or marinaded in advance. Another method is to wrap it up like a parcel and seal it with flour and water before roasting, as in the following recipe.

Roast Venison

a joint of venison
dripping or clarified fat
flour
water

The flour-and-water paste used in this recipe is called a huff paste and protects the flesh from too harsh cooking. Basting serves to cook the paste and through it the meat—if the basting is omitted the paste will crack and the meat become dry. The paste is not eaten.

Rub the meat all over with clarified fat or dripping.

Make sufficient stiff flour-and-water paste to completely enclose the joint. Wrap again in greaseproof paper and tie with string. Roast by the 'slow roast' method in a moderate oven, 180°C (350°F, Gas Mark 4), for 3 – 4 hours, according to the size of the joint: allow 40 minutes per 450g (1 lb.), basting often.

Half an hour before serving, remove the wrappings, raise the heat of the oven, dredge the meat with flour and baste well.

Serve with brown gravy and redcurrant jelly.

Wood Pigeons with Cabbage

1 large green cabbage
6-8 rashers fat bacon
salt
pepper
1 tablespoon chopped parsley
sprig of thyme (or ½ teaspoon dried tyme)
fat for frying
1 bay leaf
2 pigeons, prepared and trussed

Blanch the cabbage in boiling water for 10 minutes. Drain, plunge into cold water and leave for 10 minutes. Drain well, pressing out as much water as possible, and chop coarsely.

Line a 900-ml (2-pint) greased flameproof casserole with the cabbage and half the bacon. Season with salt and pepper and add the parsley and thyme.

Meanwhile, have some fat very hot in a frying pan to brown the pigeons, turning them so they are browned all over. Transfer the birds to the casserole, add the bay leaf, cover with the remaining bacon and put on a close-fitting lid. Bring to the boil (there is sufficient liquid in the ingredients) and simmer for at least 2 hours.

The birds can be cut in half and served straight from their bed of cabbage in the casserole.

serves 2

Pigeon Pâté

Marinade
1 cup red wine
½ cup vinegar
1 bay leaf
1 level teaspoon dried thyme.
a grating of nutmeg
salt
pepper
4 small onions, finely chopped

3 pigeons, jointed

Pâté
meat from the marinaded
   pigeons
225 g (½ lb.) sausage meat
salt
pepper
1 slice bread, crusts removed
milk
225 g (½ lb.) bacon rashers

This is a more sophisticated recipe which was given to me by the wife of a gamekeeper on a big estate in Somerset. She used to make it for 'the big house' she told me. Young or old birds can be used.

Make a marinade of the wine, vinegar, herbs, seasoning and onions and pour it over the pigeon joints. Leave to marinate for three to four days, turning the pigeons occasionally.

To make the pâté: mince the pigeon meat twice and mix with the sausage meat. Season with salt and pepper. Soak the crumbled bread in enough milk to moisten it, then mix into the meat.

Line the bottom of an ovenproof dish (choose one with a close-fitting lid) with some of the bacon rashers. Press the meat mixture in firmly, put more bacon on top, cover with the lid and bake in a moderate oven, 190°C (375°F, Gas Mark 5), for 2-2½ hours.

This pâté will keep for 2-3 weeks in cold weather.

serves 6-8

Pot-Roast Pigeon

2 pigeons, prepared and
   trussed
seasoned flour
25g (1 oz) butter
1 level teaspoon mixed herbs

Coat the pigeons in seasoned flour and toss them in very hot butter in a large saucepan. Add the herbs, cover with a close-fitting lid and cook slowly for about 1½ hours.

Serve with the liquid in the pan slightly thickened, as gravy, and with bread sauce and chips or crisps.

serves 2

CHISSELL & SON
FAMILY BUTCHERS

OX

WETHERS

OX

Vegetables,
Soups, Salads,
Fruit
and Preserves

Vegetables, Soups, Salads,

We tend to think of the vegetables and fruit we grow or can buy in such abundance today as being known only to us, our mothers, and possibly our grandmothers. But this is not true except for such things as oranges, bananas, grapefruit and some of the more exotic vegetables like red and green peppers and aubergines. Strangely enough, although the tomato was introduced three hundred years ago, the large scale cultivation of it commercially did not start until the beginning of this century. In Flora Thompson's classic of country living, *Lark Rise to Candleford*, tomatoes were seen for the first time in the 1800s and it was said they were 'love apples' and 'nasty things that only the gentry eat'.

Thomas Tusser writing in 1550 lists the vegetables which should be planted as 'Beanes, Cabbegis, Carrets, Gourdes, Parsneps, Roncevell Peas, Rapes and Turnips'. 'Roncivell' or 'runcivell' appear to mean peas of a superior kind, though I can find no real definition. Many old cookery books refer to 'sallets', which seem to have been any variety of green vegetables rather than just the uncooked salads we know today. What we do not know is which varieties of these vegetables our ancestors grew, but it is most likely that most of them were of the small 'one crop a year' variety and certainly not the giant objects we see today at village shows. Equally certainly they were for summer consumption only—storage methods were of the most primitive kind. Root vegetables were buried in clamps or covered with sand, beans were dried or salted, peas dried, onions hung in ropes from the ceiling of the kitchen, herbs tied in bunches and hung along the beams.

Winter foods must have been dreary and unexciting two or three hundred years ago, both for man and beast, and I am continually brought up short when I think of the sheer labour of feeding a family in those conditions. What was it like, I wonder, to see the light, bright days of summer grow shorter and know that winter lay ahead; that the store of grain must last until the next harvest, that the turnips and carrots, dried beans and onions were all you would have until spring brought the new crop? Dorothy Hartley, in her vastly knowledgeable book,[1] describes vividly how the peasant woman must have felt. Autumn meant the end of all the green food from woods and commons, the last wild fruit was finished, and the corn had been gathered (they cut it high by hand, with reaping-hooks, and the cattle browsed on the straw). The geese and hens had eaten the fallen grain and

[1] Dorothy Hartley

Fruit and Preserves

been eaten in turn, the pigs had eaten the fallen acorns and beech mast, and now the pigs were killed off for winter, one by one. Winter came, and there were salt and dried meats, and some parsnips. After a good harvest these lasted well enough, but as the winter dragged out, the last of the fresh meat went; only the few beasts necessary for breeding in the spring remained.

But this was the life as lived by the peasant; the lord in his manor could be enjoying a feast which included boar's head, capons, pheasants, sturgeon, venison, peacock, perch, pigeons, quails and snipe, with 'sweetmeats' to follow.

Feast and famine were never very far apart at the time of the Black Death, the plague which is said to have killed one in five of the population, and which probably more than any single event changed the story of the English people. This plague struck at the foundation of life as it was then organized by decimating the peasant population and so giving them, through scarcity value, the upper hand over their lords and landlords. The power of the landlords had been based on large numbers of 'bound men' or 'henchmen', men who tilled the land for the owner, served in his private army when required and subsisted themselves on what little was left when the crops had been harvested.

Quoting loosely from *The Land* by John Higgs:[2]

> The most important animal was the sheep and it is clear that more milk was obtained from sheep than from cows. The milk was not drunk but was used for making butter and cheese . . . a very important protein element in the diet during the winter months. Pigs were the main providers of fresh meat, and most of their diet came from roots and nuts in the woodlands. For the humbler people geese, ducks and chickens could be kept and bees provided sugar.'

And, ominously, he goes on: 'To supplement the diet the gathering of wild harvests on the wastes was important, particularly in years of scarcity and famine . . .in two early fourteenth century years the English ate bark.'

But here, as always, although the history books and the writers tell us the foods which were grown, they never tell us how they were cooked. Thomas Tusser writes:

[2]John Higgs (ed. Jack Simmons)

Good peason and leekes, to make poredge in Lent
And peascods in July, save fish to be spent

In other words, use the old dried peas first, and when they are used up cook the pea pods to make the fish go further. His list of aromatic herbs contains 42 varieties, but in no case does he say how to use them. His advice on fruit-growing rings rather nicely:

Wife into they garden and set me a plot
With strawberry roots of the best to be got,
Such growing abroad, among thorns in the wood,
Well chosen and picked, prove excelent good.

The barbary, raspberry and gooseberry too,
Look now to be planted, as other things do,
The gooseberry, raspberry, and roses all three,
With strawberry under then trimly agree.

But I have a feeling that the mantle of Thomas Tusser has descended onto the shoulders of the modern journalist cookery writer who makes you squirm when he or she writes in October that all your Christmas cookery should have been done by now or it will not mature and your time will have been wasted. Just listen to old Thomas on the subject of when to gather your fruit:

Fruit gathered too timely will taste of the wood
will shrink and be bitter, and seldom prove good
So fruit that is shaken, and best off a tree
with bruising in falling, soon faulty will be

Just because the history books don't tell us much, any little snippet we can pick up from old diaries or commonplace books has to be treasured, and sometimes folklore can be of more than passing interest. The Tamar valley is said to have been smothered in cherry trees at one time; why did they die away? Were the cherries too much of a target for the birds, was the season too short, the crop too difficult to pick? No one seems able to tell me. I myself have seen the damson trees of Dittisham in full bloom all up the little valley, but the local people say there is not much demand today, and many of the older trees yield only blossom.

Yet local tales sometimes get sudden unexpected confirmation. A local paper carried an article about 'the mazard . . . a fruit like a black cherry' which had all but died out but which a local nurseryman had decided to re-propagate and of which he would soon have some trees ready to sell. One of my dictionaries had never heard the word, but then in very small print in an ancient copy of *Chambers* which I bought, I believe, for twopence - I saw 'Mazard, a black cherry, once grown in North Devon'.

Two twentieth-century developments are of particular interest in the south-west. First, the expansion of already existing watercress beds in Dorset, which is now the fourth largest production area for this most delectable of green salads; and secondly, the rise of the 'pick-it-yourself' nursery garden and orchard. The fresh clear water from artesian wells in the chalky Dorset countryside is ideal for the growing of commercial crops of watercress (though the selling of it is largely done in the big conurbations like Birmingham and Manchester). The difficulties of transportation have been largely overcome by the use of chiller tanks and fast carriage so that cress picked one day in Dorset reaches the markets of the big cities by the next morning.

The growth of 'pick-it-yourself' fruit and vegetable outlets is due to a combination of various factors; the high cost of labour for picking, the increased demand by the housewife with the new capacity to store large quantities in her deep freeze, and also the greater mobility of the family since the increase in car ownership. More and more nursery gardens and orchards are opening their premises to people who turn up in their thousands to pick everything from strawberries to potatoes. A development which seems to benefit all concerned.

Here in the south-west, holiday makers regard the outing to pick their own fruit and vegetables as akin to the old hay-making, for which no amateur help is now needed, and they turn out in answer to the newspaper advertisements which regularly display fruits available and times for picking, or they see the notice chalked, on a board in the hedge, which says, 'Picking Today - Strawberries'. I still cherish the memory of a small, rather crooked notice board, propped up in a hedge, which proudly proclaimed *'Picking Today Plums'*, and underneath the legend *'Rabbit's Milk'*.

Thinking of fruit brings me to jam. The method of producing jam used by the big manufacturers has been adopted because—as must be obvious—fruit only comes once a year and is then available for only short periods. So the fruit is stored in enormous tanks, having had chemicals added to make it keep, then, during the rest of the year, the contents of the tanks are turned into jam, with artificial colouring put in to replace what the chemicals take out. A permitted amount of 'other raw materials' is also added. I stress 'permitted' because it is perfectly legal, and the result is value for money, if slightly too sweet and gooey for many of us. But commercially produced jam is not really at all like what we get when we make it ourselves. In the recipe section you will find some old country methods which will give rich-tasting, satisfying results.

Honey (although strictly speaking not classifiable under fruit at all) follows naturally from jam and is one of the nicest products of the countryside, and also one of the oldest. It was the principle sweetener until the eighteenth century.

Dorset to me always spells honey; once we found—hidden in one of the deep coombes climbing up from the Blackmore Vale—a honey farm with row upon row of hives, half-hidden by a sudden curve in the hill, and one of our small sons, enraptured by the sight, pointed and said, 'Look, honey huts!', which they have been for me ever since.

West Country bee-keepers have wisely formed themselves into an association which monitors the quality of the product of its members, and people come back again and again for what is probably the oldest form of processed food in the world.

Honey can be used in many cake recipes and makes the best sweetener for fruit that I know, if a trifle expensive. When using honey for cakes, remember that it is more liquid than the same amount of sugar, so allow for this and reduce the quantity of mixing liquid accordingly.

VEGETABLES

Carrot Chips

large carrots, cooked
beaten egg
fat for deep frying
parsley, finely chopped

Cut the carrots as you would potatoes for chips. Dip them in beaten egg and deep fry in slightly smoking fat. Drain well and dredge with parsley before serving.

Cauliflower Fritters

1 cauliflower
batter for coating
fat for deep frying
100g (¼ lb.) grated cheese

Wash the cauliflower and boil until tender. Drain and leave to cool. When it is cold, divide into florets, dip each in batter, then fry in hot deep fat. Drain well, sprinkle with cheese and serve at once.

Cornish Potato Cake

450g (1 lb.) freshly boiled
    potatoes
25g (1 oz) butter
100g (¼ lb.) flour
salt

These are not, strictly speaking, the tetti cakes of the West Country. Tetti cake recipes come from both Devon and Cornwall and often contain sugar, dried fruit and/or candied peel. They can be found in the Bread and Cakes section (p. 115).

While they are still hot, mash the potatoes with the butter, mixing well. Stir in the flour slowly and add salt to taste.

Roll the paste out very thinly on a floured board and cut out rounds about the size of a saucer. Slide these onto a hot girdle or greased frying pan, prick the surface with a fork and cook for 3 minutes on each side. Serve hot.

serves 2

Devonshire Breakfast Dish

It is the custom in Devonshire to re-cook the potatoes left over from the day before in the pan in which the breakfast bacon has been fried and to serve the two together.

The potato is mashed and seasoned with salt and pepper. It is then turned into the hot bacon fat, stirred about over the fire, pressed down into a thick cake, well browned underneath and then turned out brown side uppermost onto a hot dish. The crisp curls of bacon are placed on and around it, or in a separate dish.

Devonshire Stew

450g (1 lb.) potatoes, boiled
225g (½ lb.) cabbage, boiled
225g (½ lb.) onions, boiled
(changing water twice
during cooking)
salt
pepper
good beef dripping or butter

Dice the potatoes, shred the cabbage and chop the onions. Mix these together and season well.

Heat a lump of dripping or butter in a frying pan and brown the vegetables well. Serve hot.

serves 4

Likky Pie

12 small leeks
225g (½ lb.) green bacon
salt
pepper
1 cup milk
350g (¾ lb.) suet crust
2 eggs, separated
75ml (3 fl. oz) cream

Wash and trim the leeks and cut in small pieces. Scald in boiling water for 5 minutes.

Cut the bacon in very thin slices. Put a layer of bacon in the bottom of a 20-cm (8-inch) pie dish, then a layer of leeks and continue the layers, seasoning each, until the dish is almost full and the ingredients are used up. Pour in the milk and cover the dish with the suet crust. Bake in a moderate oven, 180°C (350°F, Gas Mark 4), for an hour.

Meanwhile, beat the yolks and whites of the eggs separately (the whites should form peaks) and when the pie is cooked, lift off the crust gently, pour the milky liquid from the dish and substitute the cream and eggs. Replace the crust and serve the pie hot (the heat of the dish will cook the eggs sufficiently without further time in the oven).

serves 6

Onion and Apple Pie

225g (½ lb.) shortcrust pastry
450g (1 lb.) apples
225g (½ lb.) onions

'Line a shallow tin [26.5cm x 14cm (10½ x 5½inches)] with thin shortcrust and cover the bottom with a layer of peeled, cored and finely sliced apple. Cover this with a layer of onion rings, sprinkle with a teaspoonful of finely chopped sage, pepper, salt and a pinch of mixed spice. Go on with alternate layers till the top is reached, which pile up fairly high. Moisten the edge of the paste and put scraps of butter (or Cornish cream) on top of the top layer. Cover with a thin crust and bake in a brisk oven— or under a bake-pot. To be eaten hot.

Some do put a little sugar over the apples if they be very sour—but 'tis better not.'[3]

serves 4 – 5

[3] *Cornish Recipes*

Onion Charlotte

1kg (2 lb.) onions, peeled
575ml (1 pint) milk
275ml (½ pint) water
salt
black pepper
½ teaspoon mace
a good pinch cinnamon
5-6 slices bread, crusts
  removed
50g (2 oz) butter (approx.)
25g (1 oz) cornflour
1 tablespoon grated cheese
2 tablespoons fine
  breadcrumbs, fresh

Cook the onions in boiling water until they are almost tender. Drain off the cooking water and add the milk and fresh water to the onions in the pan with the seasonings. Simmer until the onions are tender.

Fry the bread in as much of the butter as needed. Drain off surplus butter and line a 900-ml (2-pint) pie dish with the bread.

Strain the onion liquid into a bowl, use a little of it to slake the cornflour, then thicken all the liquid with the cornflour over a gentle heat. Pour the liquid over the sliced onions in the lined pie dish. Mix together the cheese and breadcrumbs and sprinkle them over the dish. Dot with butter and bake at 180°C (350°F, Gas Mark 4), for about 25 minutes or until the topping is well browned.

serves 4 as a main dish

Deep Fried Onions

Parts of North Cornwall were famous for their onions and fried onions were always served on special occasions.

Heat a pan of deep fat while you slice onions fairly thinly, separating the rings and tossing them in flour. Shake off any surplus flour.

Test the fat by lowering a slice of raw potato into the pan in the basket—when the fat seethes around the potato it is the correct temperature. Putting a few onion rings at a time into the basket, fry them until they are just golden brown and crisp. Drain well and transfer to a warm serving dish in the oven while the remaining onions are being cooked.

Onion Flan

shortcrust pastry to line a
  18-cm (7-inch) tin
425ml (¾ pint) thick white
  sauce
1 cup boiled chopped onion
3 tablespoons grated Cheddar
  cheese
1 tablespoon chopped parsley
1 tomato, sliced

Make a flan filling by stirring the onion, 2 tablespoons of cheese and the parsley into the sauce. Pour the filling into the pastry case, garnish with tomato slices and the remaining cheese and bake in a moderate oven, 190°C (375°F, Gas Mark 5), for half an hour.

Serve hot or prepare in advance and heat through when required.

serves 4

Turnip Pie

4 young turnips
salt
pepper
1 teacup milk
1 teacup fresh breadcrumbs
1 heaped tablespoon grated
  cheese

Wash the turnips and put them in a large pan of slightly salted boiling water. Cook for about half an hour or until they are almost tender. Drain, peel and cut them in thin slices.

Lay the slices in a 24-cm (9½-inch) pie dish and sprinkle with salt and pepper. Pour over the milk and cover first with the breadcrumbs and then cheese. Bake in a hot oven, 230°C (450°F, Gas Mark 8), until the topping is nicely browned.

serves 2

Vegetable Roly-Poly

225g (½ lb.) suet crust
gravy powder
3 carrots, peeled and grated
3 parsnips, peeled and grated
1 small turnip, peeled and
  grated
3 potatoes, peeled and sliced
3 tomatoes, sliced
salt
pepper

Roll out the suet crust fairly thinly and sprinkle gravy powder over it. Lay the carrots, parsnips, turnip and potatoes evenly over the crust. Cover with a layer of the tomatoes and season well. Roll up in a cloth and boil for 2½ hours. Serve steaming hot with a little good gravy.

serves 4

SOUPS

Cauliflower Soup

1 medium-to-large cauliflower
50g (2 oz) butter
25g (1 oz) flour
275ml (½ pint) milk
salt
black pepper

Divide the cauliflower into florets but keep the stalk and small leaves also. Cook all these in well-salted water, removing the florets as soon as they are tender and leaving the rest until cooked.

Melt the butter in a large saucepan and fry the florets very gently, taking care not to let them brown. Remove from the pan, draining off excess butter, and set aside. Stir the flour into the butter, then add 275ml (½ pint) of strained cauliflower water. Stir until thickened, then add the milk and bring to the boil. Draw the pan off the heat, test for seasoning and adjust as necessary.

Add the florets, sieve or liquidize the rest of the stalk and add this to the soup also. Serve very hot.

serves 4

Potato and Watercress Soup

1kg (2 lb.) potatoes, peeled
2 medium onions, peeled and
 chopped
275ml (½ pint) milk
salt
black pepper
2 bunches watercress, washed,
 picked over and chopped
 finely

Cook the potatoes and the onions together in boiling water until both are tender (if necessary remove the potatoes first while the onions finish cooking). Sieve or liquidize both together, turn the purée into a saucepan, add the milk and plenty of seasoning and heat through. Just before serving add the watercress.

serves 3

Mushroom Soup

50g (2 oz) butter
50g (2 oz) flour
575ml (1 pint) milk
225g (½ lb.) mushrooms,
 washed
575ml (1 pint) water
4-6 bacon rinds
salt
black pepper

Melt the butter in a large saucepan, then stir in the flour and cook for a few minutes. Add the milk, stirring until the sauce comes to the boil.

Meanwhile in a separate pan cook the mushrooms in the water with a few bacon rinds and seasoning—they will need about 5 minutes' gentle simmer. Strain the cooking water into a bowl, discard the bacon rinds and chop the mushrooms, including stalks unless they are too tough, in which case liquidize them.

Stir the mushroom liquor into the white sauce, add the mushrooms, test for seasoning and serve very hot.

serves 6

Green Pea Soup

575 ml (1 pint) of podded peas
 (old ones can be used)
25g (1 oz) butter
25g (1 oz) flour
275ml (½ pint) milk
salt
pepper
stock or water (see method)
2 tablespoons tender peas,
 cooked
1 tablespoon fine dice of
 cucumber

Simmer the peas in salted water until quite soft, drain and then put them through a sieve.

Make a sauce with the butter, flour and milk, add the pea purée, stir well and test for seasoning. This makes a very thick soup and if you prefer it thinner, add water or stock to the required consistency.

The tender peas and cucumber dice added just before serving enhance both appearance and flavour.

serves 4

Tomato Soup

1 medium onion, peeled and
  chopped
575ml (1 pint) water (approx.)
450g (1 lb.) ripe tomatoes
salt
black pepper
25g (1 oz) butter
25g (1 oz) flour
275-575ml (½-1 pint) milk
  (optional, see method)

Cook the onion in the water for 15 minutes, then add the tomatoes and seasoning and simmer until the tomatoes are very soft. Strain the cooking water into a bowl and sieve the onion and tomatoes to a purée.

Melt the butter in a large saucepan, stir in the flour, then add 275ml (½ pint) or 575ml (1 pint) of the tomato water, or of milk if you prefer, the quantity depending upon the consistency required – 275ml (½ pint) gives a thick soup. Stir in the tomato purée and heat the soup through, adjusting seasoning as necessary. If milk is used, make sure the soup does not boil again as it may curdle.

Serves 3-4

SALLADINGS

Salad Dressing

This dressing is very quickly made and will keep in a jam jar in a cool place for about 3 months.

Prepare a teaspoonful of mustard, mix in a teaspoonful of caster sugar, another of olive oil, four of evaporated milk, four of cream or top of milk, 2 tablespoons of vinegar and a good pinch of salt. Shake or stir well before use.

Cornish Curds

1 medium-to-large
  close-flowered cauliflower
275ml (½ pint) white wine
  vinegar
salad dressing (see above)

Separate the cauliflower into florets and cook in boiling salted water until just tender. Drain well and then pour over the vinegar which has been brought just to boiling point. Set aside to cool, then remove the cauliflower from the vinegar, arrange the florets on a serving dish and mask with the dressing.

Cucumber Relish

1 cucumber
½ cup olive oil
2 tablespoons white vinegar
½ clove garlic (optional)
1 teaspoon salt
½ teaspoon black pepper

Peel and slice the cucumber thinly and lay it in layers on a shallow dish. Blend all the remaining ingredients in a blender or beat extremely well with a whisk. Pour this dressing over the cucumber and set aside to chill for several hours.

Spring Salad

2-3 small lettuces
2 or 3 good sprigs of new mint
1 teaspoon sugar
a sprinkle of vinegar

Make this salad before your lettuces have much heart. There is nothing to compare with the fresh taste of spring that it brings.

Wash and drain the lettuces but keep them whole. Chop the mint and while chopping add the sugar and vinegar, turning the mint over on the chopping board as you work.

Put the lettuces into a serving dish and sprinkle the mint over, turning the lettuces gently to spread evenly. Leave to stand for at least 15 minutes before serving.

Broad Bean Salad

1kg (2 lb.) shelled broad beans
1 level teaspoon French
  mustard
1 heaped teaspoon paprika
  powder
½ teaspoon salt
black pepper
1 dessertspoon chopped
  parsley
1 tablespoon tarragon vinegar
vegetable oil

Cook the beans in slightly salted boiling water, drain well and remove the skins. Chill thoroughly.

Meanwhile, prepare the dressing by mixing together—ideally in a wooden bowl—the mustard, paprika, salt, pepper, parsley, and vinegar and enough oil to make a smooth, thin paste.

Roll the beans in the dressing and serve with cold meats.

Egg and Pea Salad

450g (1 lb.) freshly shelled
  peas
4 freshly cooked hard-boiled
  eggs
275ml (½ pint) good salad
  dressing (see page 83)

Cook the peas in a little boiling salted water for 4 minutes, draining them while they are still firm. Shell the eggs and chop them in small pieces. Mix the peas and eggs and while both are still warm pour over the salad dressing. Set aside to chill and serve very cold.

HERBS

Herby Pie

2 handfuls parsley sprigs
12 chives
3 or 4 borage leaves
1 handful lettuce hearts
1 handful spinach
1 handful mustard and cress
1 handful white beet leaves
salt
pepper

batter
5 tablespoons flour
pinch of salt
2 eggs
milk to mix

175g (6 oz) good shortcrust
    pastry (optional, see
    method)

Wash the herbs and vegetables well and cook in boiling water for 3 or 4 minutes. Drain thoroughly, then chop them well. Spread the chopped mixture in a 22-cm (8½-inch) buttered pie dish (the dish can be lined with pastry if preferred) and season.

Make the batter by mixing the sifted flour and salt with the eggs and sufficient milk to make the consistency of thick cream. Pour the batter over the herbs, stir together gently, then bake in a moderate oven, 190°C (375°F, Gas Mark 5), for 35 minutes.

serves 4

Minty Pie

225g (½ lb.) shortcrust pastry
4-5 eggs
½ cup chopped mint
salt
pepper

Line a 20-cm (8-inch) baking tin with two-thirds of the pastry. Break the eggs onto this carefully, top with the mint, season well and cover with the remaining pastry.

Brush the top with beaten egg and bake at 220°C (425°F, Gas Mark 7) for 25-30 minutes. Serve hot or cold.

serves 4

Faggot of Herbs

Tie together some sprigs of mint, parsley, thyme, rosemary and marjoram and leave enough spare string to secure around the lid or handle of the cooking pot. After use, remove from the pot, drain and store in a dry place. The faggot can be used several times until the flavour fades.

(If you have no fresh herbs use dried ones in a small muslin or nylon bag—like a bouqet garni. Dry the bag well after use by hanging in a warm place.)

FRUIT

Gingered Pear Pudding

450g (1 lb.) pears (hard ones can be used)
25g (1 oz) chopped preserved ginger
granulated sugar to taste
100g (¼ lb.) fresh breadcrumbs, white or brown
50g (2 oz) shredded suet

Peel and core the pears and slice finely. Add the ginger and sugar to taste, then mix together gently without breaking the pear slices.

Mix the breadcrumbs and suet. Butter a 850-ml (1½-pint) pudding basin and fill it with alternate layers, each about 2½ cm (1 inch) thick, of pear and breadcrumbs, finishing with crumbs. Cover with buttered greaseproof paper and a cloth and steam for about 2 hours.

serves 5–6

Raisin and Rhubarb Tart

450g (1 lb.) shortcrust pastry
1 tablespoon syrup
½ cup coarse oatmeal
450g (1 lb.) young rhubarb, washed and trimmed
1 cup raisins

Line a 25-cm (10-inch) tart tin with two-thirds of the pastry.

Slightly warm the syrup in a basin over hot water, then mix in the oatmeal. Spread this mixture over the bottom of the pastry case.

Cut the rhubarb into 2½-cm (1-inch) lengths and spread evenly over the oatmeal, then sprinkle the raisins on top. Cover with a thin crust of the remaining pastry.

Bake at 180–200°C (350–400°F, Gas Mark 4–6) for 25–30 minutes until the pastry is golden. Serve hot or cold.

serves 6

Dorset Blackcurrant Bake

450g (1 lb.) shortcrust pastry
450g (1 lb.) blackcurrants, topped and tailed
sugar to taste (see method)
50g (2 oz) stoned dates, chopped finely
1 cup fresh breadcrumbs

Line a 25-cm (10-inch) tart tin with three-quarters of the pastry.

Cook the blackcurrants in a little water until they are very soft, adding some sugar if they are unusually sour, but the dates will normally give enough sweetness. Add the dates and breadcrumbs to the fruit, stir well and set aside for a few minutes until the crumbs have absorbed the juice.

Fill the pastry case with this mixture, cover with a thin crust of the remaining pastry, brush over with water and then sprinkle on caster sugar. Bake at 150°C (300°F, Gas Mark 2) for about 30 minutes until golden. Serve hot or cold.

serves 6

Blackberry Snow

1kg (2 lb.) blackberries
25g (1 oz) granulated sugar
1 tablespoon gelatine
2 tablespoons syrup
white of 1 egg

Cook the blackberries with the sugar, but with no water, until the juice begins to run. Turn them into a hair sieve and press out the juice with a wooden spoon.

Slake the gelatine with a little cold water, then stir in the blackberry juice and heat gently, stirring constantly, until the gelatine is dissolved. Continue to heat until just below boiling, draw off the stove and add the syrup. Put aside in a cool place and when the mixture is beginning to set, fold in the beaten egg white. Turn into individual glass dishes or a mould and put in a cool place until completely set.

serves 4

Apple Cream

450g (1 lb.) cooking apples
225g (½ lb.) clotted cream (or a tin of condensed milk)

Peel and core the apples and grate them straight into the cream, stirring frequently to coat the apple and prevent it discolouring. Serve immediately.

This dish is, of course, infinitely better made with clotted cream rather than condensed milk, but in passing perhaps I should tell the story of one old countryman of our acquaintance who had worked on the same farm for a good many years and had his daily 'llowance of a pint of milk. As he got older the boss told him he need not come in on Sundays, and soon after this the farmer's wife asked how they did for milk on Sundays and would he like to take two pints on Saturdays. He replied, 'Oh no, thank 'ee Missus, on Sundays me and the missus has a treat—we opens a tin.'

Apple Crisps

450g (1 lb.) sharp cooking apples
50g (2 oz) butter
100g (¼ lb.) granulated sugar
4 thick slices white or brown bread, cut in cubes

Peel, core and dice the apples. Meanwhile set the butter to melt in a heavy frying pan.

Cook the apples and sugar gently in the butter until the juice begins to run. Lift the apples from the pan with a perforated slice, allowing excess butter to drain back into the pan. Keep the apples warm in a covered serving dish.

Fry the cubes of bread in the frying pan until they are golden and have soaked up all the butter. Mix the bread with the cooked apple, dredge with caster sugar and serve at once, with cream if possible.

serves 4

JAMS

Apple Jelly

This recipe is particularly good for stored fruit as little natural pectin is needed for a good result and after some months the pectin content of stored fruit is low. But new apples can be used. Use any apples from the store, allowing the juice of two lemons and the rind of one to each 1kg (2 lb.) of fruit, weighed after peeling and coring.

Cut the apples in cubes and put them in a pan with the lemon juice and grated rind. Add just enough water to cover and bring to the boil, simmering until the fruit is tender. Put in a jelly bag and leave to drip overnight.

Next day measure the liquid and allow 450g (1 lb.) sugar to each 575ml (1 pint). Put the juice and sugar in a preserving pan, bring to the boil and boil rapidly for 20 – 25 minutes until the jelly will wrinkle when tested on a saucer.

Pot and cover at once.

Apple and Ginger Jam

2¾ kg (6 lb.) apples
1.1 litres (2 pints) water
rind and juice of 4 lemons *or* 2
    level teaspoons citric or
    tartaric acid
2 teaspoons ground ginger or
    225g (½ lb.) crystalized
    ginger, chopped
2¾ kg (6 lb.) sugar

Peel, core and cut up the apples, setting aside the peel and cores and tying them in muslin.

Put the apples and water in a preserving pan with the grated rind and the juice of the lemons (or the acid) and the ginger if *ground* ginger is used. Tie the muslin bag so that it hangs in the fruit. Cook until the apples are tender. Remove the bag of peel, squeezing out any juice first.

Add the sugar, and crystallized ginger if used, and stir until the sugar dissolves. Boil quickly for about 35 minutes until the jam starts to set when tested.

These quantities yield 4½ kg (10 lb.) jam if ground ginger is used and 4¾ kg (10½ lb.) with crystallized ginger.

Bramble Jelly

3.6kg (8 lb.) blackberries
juice of 3 lemons *or* 2 teaspoons
    citric acid
850ml (1½ pints) water
450g (1 lb) sugar per 575ml
    (1 pint) of juice

Wash the blackberries and put them in a pan with the lemon juice or acid and the water. Simmer until tender. Mash well and strain through a jelly bag overnight.

Measure the juice, bring it to the boil in a preserving pan and then add the sugar. Stir well, then boil rapidly for about 25 minutes until a set is obtained on testing. Pot immediately.

These quantities yield approximately 5½kg (12 lb.) of jelly.

Lemon Curd

4 lemons
5 eggs
100 g (¼ lb.) butter
450g (1 lb.) sugar

Wash and dry the lemons, grate the rind very finely and squeeze all the juice. Put the rind and juice in the top of a double boiler, add the well-beaten eggs, then the butter and sugar. Heat, stirring constantly, until the sugar dissolves and the curd thickens.

Strain into small, hot, clean jars and seal at once. (Small jars should be used because the curd will go off quickly once it is opened. Do not make more than 2 – 3 months' supply at a time.)

These quantities yield approximately 675g (1½ lb.)

Mulberry and Apple Jam

1kg (2 lb.) apples, cored,
    peeled and diced
2¾kg (6 lb.) mulberries,
    washed
1 tablespoon citric acid
1.1 litres (2 pints) water
2¾kg (6 lb.) sugar

Put the apples to cook with the mulberries, acid and water in a preserving pan. Boil to a pulp. Add the sugar and simmer for 25 – 30 minutes until a set is obtained on testing. Pot while still hot.

These quantities yield approximately 4½ kg (10 lb.)

Rhubarb and Orange Preserve

1¾kg (4 lb.) rhubarb, washed
    and trimmed
juice and grated rind of 6
    oranges
1¾kg (4 lb.) sugar
½ teaspoon citric acid

Cut up the rhubarb and put it in a bowl with the orange rind and juice and the sugar. Leave for 12 hours, when enough juice will have been drawn not to need any additional liquid.

Put these ingredients into a preserving pan with the acid, bring to the boil and boil for 25-30 minutes until a set is obtained on testing. Pot at once.

These quantities yield approximately 4½ kg (10 lb.).

HONEY

Hazel Nut Honey Pancakes

100g + 2 dessertspoons (¼ lb.)
   flour
pinch of salt
1 egg
275ml (½ pint) milk
100g + 1 dessertspoon (¼ lb.)
   honey
juice of half a lemon
75g + 1 dessertspoon (3 oz)
   hazel nuts, finely chopped
caster sugar to dredge

Sieve the flour and salt into a bowl and make a well in the centre. Add the egg and enough milk to mix to a smooth creamy batter. Beat well, then stir in the rest of the milk and set aside.

Mix together the honey, lemon juice and nuts.

Heat a little lard in a small frying pan and pour in just enough batter to cover the base very thinly. Cook on one side until golden, then turn and cook the other side. Turn the pancake onto a warm plate, put a little nut mixture down the centre, fold the pancake in three, transfer it to a serving dish and keep hot. Make the remainder of the pancakes, dredge with caster sugar and serve at once.

12 small pancakes

Honey Cough Cure

100g (¼ lb.) pure honey
100g (¼ lb.) cod liver oil
juice of 3 lemons, strained
25g (1 oz) glycerine

Mix all the ingredients together thoroughly and pour into clean bottles. Shake before use.

Puddings

Puddings

Sorting through old recipes for pies and puddings, pastries and tarts, I was struck by the divide that seemed to exist between the 'quality' recipes, which the lord and his lady would have eaten, and those for the yeoman, farmer and peasant. For the former, custards, syllabubs, creams and tansies abound, all using butter and cream, eggs and cider, wine or even brandy (here I must retail that one of my Cornish cookery books calls for two shillings' worth of brandy in a recipe . . . how does one translate that into modern quantities I wonder?) At the other end of the scale were bag puddings, figgy duffs, suety rolls, batters—all good filling stuff but a thought heavy for modern tastes.

Then another comparison appears; most of the 'rich' puddings were oven-baked, most of the 'poor' ones boiled. So I leafed back through my collection of cookery books—some old, some not so old, but all portraying a way of life which is past—and another picture began to emerge. The oven as part of, or incorporated with, the kitchen fireplace did not come into existence until the 1800s, and then it arrived by way of an amalgamation of the open fire in the middle of the room and the bread oven in a corner, the open fire having only a hole in the roof for the smoke to escape and the bread oven no chimney at all.

The later version was the more sophisticated open fire with a chimney and a bread oven beside it, but not incorporated into it, hot cinders or wood simply being shovelled into the bread oven from the fire. These then became the kitchen range as we know it. Before that the bread oven was heated separately, and probably used only once a week for a mighty cook-up. For the rest of the week the cook had to make do with a wood-burning fire over which she hung her pots and pans, or the pot oven which I have described on p. 51. Joints for roasting would have been done on the spit.

The bread oven which went with the spit would have been the sort that was heated by bundles of furze or twigs, small faggots of wood being put into the interior, then lit and continually replenished until the oven was really hot. The ashes were then swept out and the baking done in the residual heat. So it is easy to see why bag pudding was the food of the peasant and not exotic creams and junkets. Something gentler was needed for them, and it is probable that until the kitchen range evolved the cook had to rely on her own ingenuity to thicken custards and set junkets without the aid of an oven.

A perfect example of how the cook managed—and also a pointer to the fact that an old collection of recipes is sometimes more revealing of social customs than any history book—is a recipe from one of my more treasured possessions, *A Book of Simples,* (Lewer, ed), thought to date from about 1700-50. This is the recipe, entitled 'To Make a White Pot' (my italics).

> Take a quart of new milk boyle in it a nutmeg quarter'd and cinnamon take out the whole spice and put in some slicit [sliced] manchet [fine white bread] and cover it close till tis cold then breake the bread with a spoon put in some eggs sugar and salt and a piece of butter the oven must be hotter then for a custard or *you may bake it on a chafing dish of coles leaving embers on an iron plate on ye top*.

This brings me back to the fact that few traditional puddings appear in our recipe books except those which either used a gentle heat or could be boiled (though that takes no account of tarts and pastries which would have been cooked at the time of the weekly bake). It is not surprising to find that most of the bag pudding recipes use local produce—apples, blackcurrants, curd cheese, potatoes. In the other class come the aristocrats of puddings; Damask Cream, Bath Syllabub, Curds and Cream, Gooseberry Tansy, Snowcream Pancakes and, culled again from my *Book of Simples*, such delights as 'To Make A Pyramid Cream':

> First wash one ounce of Icsinglass and lay it 2 days in rosewater then beat a pound of Almonds with a spoonful of rosewater Strain them with a quart of cream or new milk then put in your Icsinglass and sweeten with Sugar to your taste then boyle it on the fire till a drop will stand then put it in a dish and stir it till tis cold then put it in glasses and put it in a dish you Serve it up in and put cream to be 4 inches above the cream.

and 'To Make A Snow':

> Whip the whites of 3 eggs very well and sweeten a quart of cream and put to them then whip it together then put to it 3 quarters of a pint of white wine and as much Sack continue whiping it till it is very light and as it rises take it off and lay it on what you please.

Pastry recipes seem to be of the homely kind, using local fruit. I fancy though, that here in the south-west pastry was usually served to bolster up the first course rather than to titivate the 'afters'.

In addition to the pudding recipes in this section, see also under Cream, Cheese and Fruit sections.

Devonshire Beestings

Beestings is the name given to the first milk from a newly calved cow, and as there is usually more than the calf can drink itself there are innumerable country recipes for dealing with it. You either like it or loathe it, but no West Country cookery book would be complete without at least a mention of it.

We do not use the very first beestings after the cow has calved as it is so deep in colour.

I always test the beestings by putting a little in a dish in the oven for 45 minutes at 140°C (275°F, Gas Mark 1). If it sets too thick I put perhaps 575ml (1 pint) of milk to 1¾ l (3 pints) of beestings, or in altered proportions depending upon the thickness.

Take the beestings (or milk-and-beestings mixture), add 2 tablespoons sugar and a pinch of salt for each 575ml (1 pint), stir well, pour into a pie dish and sprinkle pudding spice over the top. Set the dish in a roasting pan and pour hot water into the pan to about halfway up the dish. Bake at no more than 150°C (300°F, Gas Mark 2) for about 20 minutes until set.

Beestings can be eaten hot or cold and can also be used in tarts, just like egg custard tart.

An early recipe for making a sweet cream reads like this: 'Boyle the cream with spice and sugar and add a dash of rosewater. When you have boyled your cream take two ladlesful of it being almost cold bruise the soft fruit together with it and season with sugared rosewater then put in your cream stirring altogether and so dish it up'[1]

Today I'm afraid you'll have to settle for something more like these.

Honeycomb Mould

25g (1 oz) gelatine *or* 1 packet jelly of any flavour
575ml (1 pint) fruit syrup *or* 150 ml (¼ pint) boiling water and cold water to complete jelly
2 eggs, separated
275ml (½ pint) milk

Dissolve the gelatine in a little of the cold syrup, bring the rest of the syrup to the boil, cool a little before mixing with the gelatine, then set aside. Stir thoroughly until the gelatine is dissolved. (If a packet is used, make up according to instructions.)

Warm the milk to blood heat, pour onto the beaten yolks, stir, return to the pan and cook gently, stirring constantly, until the mixture thickens. Remove from the heat, stir in the gelatine mixture and then fold in the stiffly beaten egg whites. Turn into an 850-ml (1½-pint) mould which has been prepared by wetting with cold water. Leave to set in a cool place.

serves 3

[1]Lewer

A Good Custard

1 egg per 575ml (1 pint) of
   milk
25g (1 oz) sugar per 575ml
   (1 pint) of milk
flavouring as desired (nutmeg,
   vanilla or almond essence)

Beat the yolk and white of egg separately and then blend them
together. Beat the egg into the milk. Sweeten, flavour and then
pour into a pie dish. Set the dish in a roasting pan and pour hot
water into the pan to halfway up the dish. Bake in a slow oven
140°C (275°F, Gas Mark 1), for an hour.
   575ml (1 pint) of milk makes enough custard to serve 4.

A Boiled Custard

For each 575ml (1 pint) of milk:
25g (1 oz) cornflour
25g (1 oz) butter
25g (1 oz) sugar
1 egg

Slake the cornflour with a little of the milk, then stir in the
remainder of the milk and bring to the boil. Add the butter, sugar
and any flavouring you like. Remove the pan from the heat and
add the well-beaten egg (the heat of the mixture will cook the
egg). Serve hot.

Curds and Cream

1 teaspoon lemon juice
575ml (1 pint) cold milk
150ml (¼ pint) Cornish cream
1 teaspoon caster sugar

Add the lemon juice to the milk. Heat with great care, very
slowly—without boiling—until a curd forms. Filter through a
muslin cloth to allow the liquid whey to drain through. Set in a
cool place but do not refrigerate. Serve the curds with the cream
and caster sugar.

serves 6

Devonshire Junket

1 tablespoon brandy or rum
¼ teaspoon ground cinnamon
1 tablespoon caster sugar
575ml (1 pint) of new milk (or
fresh milk)
1 teaspoon essence of rennet
75–100 ml (3–4 fl. oz) clotted
   cream

Mix together in a 850-ml (1½ pint) glass bowl the brandy,
cinnamon and sugar. Pour on the new milk, or fresh milk heated
to the temperature of new milk, about 36°C (98°F), and add the
rennet. Stir well and allow to stand until set (unlike jelly, it
will set better and more quickly at room temperature than in a
cold larder). When set, spread clotted cream over the top and
sprinkle with a little castor sugar.
   When well made, junket should cut into smooth, shiny slices
like jelly.

serves 5 – 6

Lemon Soufflé

25g (1 oz) gelatine *or* 1 packet
   lemon jelly
575ml (1 pint) lemon syrup
   (juice of 2 lemons, 425ml
   (¾ pint) water, 50g (2 oz)
   sugar) *or* 425ml (¾ pint)
   water if packet used
1 egg white
150ml (¼ pint) double cream
chopped pistachio nuts to
   decorate
green and black grapes to
   decorate

If using packet jelly, make it up with 425ml (¾ pint) hot water and set aside to cool until almost set.

If using gelatine, soak the gelatine in a little of the cold water until quite dissolved. Bring the rest of the water, the lemon juice and sugar to the boil and boil for 3 minutes. Pour this syrup onto the gelatine, stirring very thoroughly until the mixture begins to thicken.

When the jelly or gelatine is almost set, whisk well. Beat the egg white stiffly, add it to the whipped jelly and continue beating for a few minutes. Add the cream and whip the mixture until it is thick.

Pour into a prepared 1.1-litre (2-pint) soufflé dish surrounded with a collar of greaseproof paper projecting 5 cm (2 inches) above the rim.

When the soufflé is completely set, carefully remove the collar and decorate in the traditional manner with the pistachio nuts round the side and halved grapes on top.

serves 4 – 5

Mincemeat and Almond Delight

pastry
125g + 2 dessertspoons (5 oz)
   self-raising flour
pinch of salt
50g + ½ dessertspoon (2 oz)
   butter
25g (1 oz) lard
1 egg yolk
½ teaspoon lemon juice
1 tablespoon cold water

filling
50g (2 oz) butter
50g (2 oz) caster sugar
2 eggs
50g (2 oz) ground almonds
almond essence
4 tablespoons mincemeat
2 bananas
almonds, blanched and halved,
   for decoration

Sieve the flour and salt into a basin, then lightly rub in the butter and lard. Beat the egg yolk, add the lemon juice and water and gradually work into the flour, mixing to a stiff paste and adding more water if required.

For the filling, cream the butter and sugar, then stir in the beaten eggs, ground almonds and almond essence and mix well.

Line a 25-cm (10-inch) pie dish with the pastry and almost fill it with alternate layers of mincemeat and sliced bananas. Spread the almond mixture on top and decorate with halved almonds. Bake in a hot oven, 220°C (425°F, Gas Mark 7), for 30 minutes. Serve hot or cold.

serves 6

Damson Caramel Pudding

50g (2 oz) margarine or butter
75-100g (3-4 oz) granulated
　sugar
4 slices dry bread, about ½ –
　cm (¼ – inch) thick
450g (1 lb.) ripe damsons,
　halved and stoned

This was a special Dittisham recipe, the village being famous for its damsons. Any variety of plum can be used instead.

Spread the sides and base of a 850-ml (1½-pint) pie dish with margarine and sprinkle liberally with sugar. Line the dish neatly with the bread, covering the sides and base completely.

Put a layer of damsons in the dish, sprinkle with sugar, add another layer of bread and then more damsons and sugar. Finish the top with neat slices of bread, dot over with margarine and cover with a piece of buttered greaseproof paper.

Bake in a moderately hot oven, 200°C (400°F, Gas Mark 6), for an hour. Turn out onto a hot dish and serve with milk.

serves 4

Devonshire Gooseberry Tart

450g (1 lb.) gooseberries,
　topped and tailed
2 tablespoons water
100g (¼ lb.) granulated sugar
lemon essence
1 egg, separated
250g (9 oz) shortcrust pastry
1 tablespoon caster sugar

Cook the gooseberries gently with the water and granulated sugar until soft. Mash them to a pulp and flavour with lemon essence. Set aside to cool and then stir in the beaten egg yolk.

Meanwhile, line a 23-cm (9-inch) sandwich tin with two-thirds of the pastry rolled to about ½cm (¼inch) thick. Pour in the gooseberry pulp and close the tart with a round of thinner pastry rolled from the remainder. Make two cuts in the form of a cross in the centre of the tart. Bake in a hot oven 230°C (450°F, Gas Mark 8), for 20 minutes until the pastry is golden.

Finally whisk the egg white to a stiff froth, spread it over the top of the tart and spinkle with caster sugar. Put back in the oven for 3 minutes. Serve hot or cold with clotted Devon cream.

serves 5 – 6

Mixed Fruit Stirabout

100g (¼ lb.) flour
pinch of salt
50g (2 oz) butter
50g (2 oz) sugar
2 breakfastcups fruit
275ml (½ pint) milk (approx.)

This is an old farmhouse recipe and can be used for all kinds of fresh fruit—rhubarb, gooseberries, currants, raspberries, etc.—alone or mixed.

Sieve the flour and salt into a bowl and cut the butter into the flour in small pieces, but do not rub it in. Add the sugar and prepared fruit (if rhubarb, cut in small cubes). Mix with milk to the consistency of a thick batter, pour into a 20-cm (8-inch) overnproof dish and bake in a hot oven, 220°C (425°F, Gas Mark 7), for about 30 minutes. Serve with sugar and thick cream.

serves 5

October Cobbler

approx. 1 litre (1 quart)
    blackberries
3½ tablespoons caster sugar
1 tablespoon lemon juice
½ cup water
2 tablespoons butter
2 cups flour
4 teaspoons baking powder
1 teaspoon salt
5 tablespoons lard
2½ tablespoons milk

Wash the berries and put them in a 23-cm (9-inch) buttered pie dish. Sprinkle with 2 tablespoons of sugar, the lemon juice and water. Dot over the butter.

Sift the flour with the baking powder and salt and rub the lard in lightly. Stir in the remaining sugar and the milk and roll out the pastry to the size of the pie dish. Cover the fruit with the pastry lid, neatening the edges (which must not come over the side of the dish), and prick with a fork. Bake in a hot oven, 220°C (425°F, Gas Mark 7), for 30 minutes and serve hot with custard sauce or cream.

serves 6

Transparent Tart

100g (¼ lb.) unsalted butter
100g (¼ lb.) caster sugar
4 eggs, well-beaten
1 teaspoon grated nutmeg
18-cm (7-inch) flan case lined
    with shortcrust pastry

'Put butter, sugar and eggs into a pan. Stir over the fire until of a "scrambled egg" consistency. Put in a basin and mix in a teaspoonful of grated nutmeg. Bake in a flan case lined with pastry. Sprinkle with caster sugar before serving'[2]

The tart will take about 35 minutes in a moderate oven, 180°C (350°F, Gas Mark 4).

serves 5-6

'To Make A Tansy, of the Finer Sort'

'Take 16 eggs, all but 6 whites, beat them very well, put into them some sugar and sack, then beat them again, then put a pint of cream boyling Colour it with the juice of the Spinage, green wheat or prime rose leaves, mix it well and sweeten it to your taste, so let it stand till you need it. Strew on Sugar and Garnish with orange or lemon [peel].'[3]

And if this is beyond most of us today, try the next recipe which is still an old one, dated about 1700.

[2]Nell Heaton
[3]Lewer

Gooseberry Tansy

'Cook a quart of gooseberries with some butter in a covered jar till quite soft, beat 4 eggs and fill them with a double handful of fine white breadcrumbs and a cupful of sugar. Blend this into a gooseberry pulp over a slow heat, stirring gently till the mass is cooked firm (on no account let it get too hot or the custard will curdle).

Turn out onto a hot dish, sprinkle with crushed sugar, and serve with hot cider or melted apple jelly . . .

The completed dish should be the consistency of a "solid omelette". Raspberries make a good tansy, and so do mulberries and loganberries. Strawberries are delicious, and should be laced with a little white wine before serving. Apple is good served with blackberry syrup.'[4]

[4]Dorothy Hartley

Bread, Cakes and Biscuits

Bread, Cakes and Biscuits

Thirty years ago, when we first came to Devon and to farming, we found behind the bricked-up wall of our sitting-room an old bread oven, complete except for the door. The inside was of beautiful smooth brick, but in my ignorance I could not see how to get it hot. All my neighbours in the village could tell me was that you put a faggot in and you lit it and then when the oven was hot you baked your bread. As cooking instructions these seemed to leave something unsaid, but then, amongst a collection of almost forgotten books in an antiquarian bookseller's in Exeter, I found a very tattered little book entitled *Bread by Anonymous* and in it was this:

To heat a brick oven, with wood.

Lay a quantity of shavings or light brushwood in the centre of the oven and some small branches of faggot wood upon them, over these place as many of the larger branches as will make a tolerably large fire and set light to them. As the wood consumes keep adding to it throwing in stout pieces of faggot and lastly two or three moderate logs. From one to two hours will be required to heat the brick thoroughly, towards the end of the time the fire which till now has been in the centre should be spread all over the floor of the oven so that the whole floor may be heated evenly.

When the fire is burnt out and the red glowing ceases scrape out the charcoal letting it drop through the slot at the oven door and brush out the small ash with a broom of twigs. Then take a large clean mop, dip it in hot water and mop over every part of the inside of the oven clearing out the last of the dust and leaving a little steam within the oven. Leave the oven closed for some time to even the heat before you open and fill it. If the oven seems too hot it is better to close the door and leave the bread to cook evenly than to try to hurry the cooling by leaving the door open as that cools unevenly and the bread will be a bad shape. Once the loaves are packed in do not open the oven door till two hours have passed and after drawing out your bread have the rest of your baking ready and shut the door instantly, and so you may go on until the oven is quite cold. Last of all put in the kindling you may want to make the fire the following week so that you may be sure it is quite dry.

Two things I find puzzling about this: first, we are always told that pastry must be cooked at a hotter temperature than bread, so when did the pies go in? And, second, our own bread oven at the farm had no dust hole, so how did you sweep it out? To neither question am I ever likely to get an answer.

To my eternal shame I never did make bread in that oven, but years later, when we had left the farm, I heard that the local baker in the village near where we now live was selling up and I managed to buy a dough trough, two standards, two peels and an old salt box, and for an explanation of these terms I cannot do better than quote again from my little book.

> The dough trough should be waist high made of elm wood, bolted together with wooden pins and secured on a thick base which forms the top of a firm legged stand. It should slant pretty finely and the inside be smooth if it has been in use some time it will have a sweet yeasty smell. This trough should not be scalded after use but wiped clear, dough sticking to the side to be crumbed off with a dry cloth. You may store your cloths baking tins and all utensils in here in between bakings . . .
>
> The standard is a round wooden flour container which when filled to the brim will hold exactly a measure of flour . . .

Useful this, but I have my doubts as to its exactness because I am fairly sure that my two wouldn't contain the same amount—one is so obviously bigger than the other—though I have never had the time nor the courage to test them out.

'The peels are flat shovel shaped pieces of metal on long wooden handles for reaching into the oven and by sliding the blade under the loaves bringing them out.'

The salt box is just what it sounds like: an oblong wooden box with a hinged lid (with encrustations of salt still along the hinge). The aspect that charms me is that the sides and top are elaborately carved. Now who, I wonder, had time to do that?

Bread more than any other food brings me face to face with the question which has dogged me all the time as I have been gathering material for this book: how exactly did they *cook* their food? Places such as the Abbot's Kitchen at Glastonbury—where enormous bread ovens are built into each of the four corners and in which we are told a huge fire burned night and day in the centre of the room—or the humble little peat and turf fires of the slate-roofed isolated Cornish farms seem a far cry from the modern Aga; yet all that has happened in the interval is that a fire has been put underneath in a fireproof box!

I was always fascinated by the history book descriptions of how fires would originally have been built in the middle of the 'hall place' or main living/eating/sleeping room, the smoke finding its way out as best it could. Then, we are told, the fire was put at the end of the house with a chimney built into the wall to take out the smoke. The bread oven developed next, but still—as is clearly shown from my old book—it was only a hole in the thickness of the wall and was heated by lighting a fire inside it, then clearing out the ash and using the residual heat. Someone then appears to have had the idea of scooping out underneath the fire to make a better draught, and by putting thick logs on top of the flames a platform was formed on which iron cooking pots could be rested before the logs burnt through. But there was still no real oven, and it is only when metal comes onto the scene that we find the first breakthrough. Here was a material which would withstand heat from underneath and would also get hot itself. While gathering recipes I have found, therefore, that the early ones are all clearly shown to have been for baking *on* or *beside* a fire, not for putting *in* an oven.

This, together with the fact that the south-west has never been one of the richest of areas, means that most of our bread-making recipes are of the simple, filling type. But we also have a bewildering variety of buns, scones and the like. Starting with splits, chudleys, cut rounds and tuff cakes (which came originally from the turf cakes of Cornish turf fires)—these all being variations of the same thing—we come to the aristocrat of buns, the Bath bun, which is still being made to the original recipe by a baker in Bath. The Sally Lunn is a plainer variation of the yeast bun, and is also made in Bath and sold piping hot and dripping with butter in the tea shop to which it gives its name.

Two recipes which I find especially interesting are the double bake and the Dorset Knob. Double bakes are small finger rolls which, like some biscuits, are put through another baking, and I suspect that they are a manifestation of the inherent carefulness of the West Country house-wife—they don't quickly become stale. You couldn't bake every day, so as well as bread you made something like double bakes which were still edible several days later. Dorset Knobs, white or brown, are small crisp rolls which are again baked twice, giving a very long life. In the recipe section I give a recipe for double bakes, but Dorset Knobs are a proprietary brand with a secret formula. The little factory at Morecombelake where they are made can be visited, and it is fascinating, reminding me of something out of Disney Land.

There is more interest in different flours today than there has been for some time. Many people hunt out wholemeal flour and those who make their own bread now buy one or other of the special bread-making flours sold under brand names. An old mill near Crewkerne (Lockyer's Clapton Mills) still grinds flour with a centuries-old waterwheel and their flour is sold locally in many shops.

When I first started a small home-made food business, I employed home bakers with considerable success; but when the new public health regulations came into force the standards demanded before a home bakery licence is awarded became so exacting and unbending that most of my bakers gave up in despair. They didn't want, or couldn't be bothered, to submit themselves and their kitchens to the required inspection. So while gaining a higher standard of hygiene, we lost a whole range of baking skills.

I make no apology for the plainness of the cake recipes I give. Cakes of the richer sort do not suit our way of life; we invented the cream tea and that needs no rich cake to follow it up. The West Country abounds in solid cut-and-come-again family cakes—the cider cake from Somerset will keep for a month or more. Vinegar cake, date cake and Sarah's cake are all no-nonsense, one-baking-day-a-week varieties, the sort you can either cut into to fill a working man's dinner bag or put before your guests without embarrassment. Recipes like these are unknown to the vast range offered by the commercial manufacturers, and you will find they are all extremely popular.

BREAD

The trouble with home bread-making is that temperatures are vital, and I am convinced that no cook is ever aware of the temperatures in her kitchen. So to say the dough should prove for a specific length of time is asking for trouble as the kitchen may be either too hot or too cold. Cookery books all say that the dough must be kept warm and that it must prove in a given time, but bread dough is really the most good-natured substance and should be handled according to kitchen conditions. I once made up three 56 lb. bags of flour into loaves working in a tent in the middle of a ploughed field with a howling gale blowing the tent flaps in our faces as we worked! And if I make bread at home I use the overnight rising method by which you mix the dough to the proving stage, then cover it and put it in a *cool* place until the next morning when it will have risen to the top of the pan.

So in all the following methods I give *suggested* times of proving, but there is no need to be distressed if yours doesn't come up in that time. The best test is to press a finger deep into the dough and if it springs back at once and feels elastic then it has proved and you can go on to the next stage.

Do buy one of the 'strong' bread-making flours: Spiller's Extras and McDougall's Country Life are ones to look for. Allinson's wholemeal is also good but makes a coarser loaf.

In all recipes either fresh or dried yeast may be used: 25g (1 oz) fresh yeast is equivalent to 15g (½ oz) dried.

Plain Breads

Beginner's Bread

675g (1½ lb.) wholemeal flour
675g (1½ lb.) plain flour
4 level teaspoons salt
1 level tablespoon syrup or
  brown sugar
1 litre (1¾ pints) lukewarm milk
  and water mixed in equal
  quantities
1 teaspoon honey
50g (2 oz) fresh yeast

Try this simple recipe if you have never made bread before. I give the methods for using fresh and dried yeast separately for clarity.

fresh yeast
Sieve the flour and salt into a warm basin, add the syrup or sugar and leave in a warm place.

Whisk the milk and water with the honey and yeast in a jug. Make a well in the centre of the flour and add the liquid, mixing to a rather stiff dough with the hands. Half fill greased bread tins (two 1kg (2 lb.) tins or four 450g (1 lb.) ones), pressing down firmly with damp fingers. Cover with a damp cloth and set to rise in a warm place away from draughts until the dough has filled the tins.

Remove the cloth, brush the tops of the loaves with milk or melted butter and bake in a preheated oven, the first 5 minutes at 230°C (450°F, Gas Mark 8), then reduce the heat to 220°C (425°F Gas Mark 7) or move to a lower shelf and cook for a further 25–30 minutes, or until ready. (Test by turning the loaf out of the tin and tapping the base—if it sounds hollow, the bread is ready, if not, put back in the oven, out of the tin, and cook for a further 5 minutes. Cool on wire racks.

dried yeast
Use 2 level teaspoons yeast and reconstitute by mixing it with a pinch of sugar, and 275ml (½ pint) of the liquid. Leave to stand for 5 minutes, then whisk until frothy before adding to the milk, water and honey.

Breakfast Bread

900g (2 lb.) flour
2 level teaspoons salt
1 teaspoon fresh yeast in
    575ml (1 pint) milk
1 teaspoon brown sugar

'Warm everything, and make and knead up as you would bread, but do not set it to rise till you finally tuck it down again in the panshon, then cover it, and leave it overnight in the warm kitchen. Next morning (not later than six o'clock) work it up into rolls and leave them to rise on the baking sheet near the stove till half an hour before breakfast, then bake in a hot oven, and serve hot, wrapped up in a warm napkin on a hot earthenware dish.'[1]

Plank Bread

900g (2 lb.) flour
1 teaspoon salt
25g (1 oz) lard
25g (1 oz) fresh yeast
1 teaspoon brown sugar
1 breakfast cup tepid milk and
    water

The 'plank' is of Welsh origin but it can also be met with in North Devon and Somerset which have very close associations with the Welsh coast through the old trading links between the smaller ports of the North Bristol Channel and the coasts of these two counties. In the West Country the plank is now called a 'baking iron' or bake sheet and is often a plain sheet of iron, or even an old frying pan with not much of a handle.

The secret of its successful use is that it should never be washed, only rubbed to clean off any fat, and should be heated until it is very hot to the finger. (Originally the plank would have been heated over a clear open fire). A standard frying pan or griddle can be used in those kitchens where there is no 'plank'.

Sift the flour and salt into a large warmed mixing bowl and set

[1]Dorothy Hartley

aside in a warm place for 5 or 10 minutes. Rub the lard into the flour. Put the yeast in a jug with the sugar and mix with the liquid.

Make a well in the centre of the flour and pour in the yeast. Mix to a soft dough, cover the bowl with a warm cloth and leave to rise for an hour in a warm place away from draughts.

Mould the dough into a large flat cake not more than an inch thick, kneading and pressing with the hands towards the edges. Leave to rise for 15 minutes.

Put the bread carefully on the heated plank and bake for 20 minutes on each side.

Serve either hot or cold.

Quick Bread

1.3kg 4 dessertspoons (3 lb.) plain flour
1 level teaspoon brown sugar
150 ml (¼ pint) boiling milk mixed with 700ml (1¼ pints) cold water
1 teaspoon honey or syrup
50g (2 oz) fresh yeast
4 level teaspoons salt

Sieve 450g (1 lb.) of the flour into a bowl, add the sugar and leave in a warm place. Mix the milk and water with the honey or syrup in a jug. Add the yeast and stir thoroughly. (If *dried yeast* is used, take ½ teacup of water from the given amount, mix it with a pinch of sugar and then sprinkle the dried yeast on top. Leave to stand for 5 minutes, then whisk as though beating eggs. Add this whisked mixture to the milk and water mixture as above.)

Add the liquid gradually to a well in the centre of the flour, mixing with a wooden spoon to a smooth batter. Beat well, cover with a cloth and stand in a warm place for a further 15 minutes. The mixture will rise and bubble.

Meanwhile sift the salt with the remaining flour. Add this flour to the batter a little at a time, at first using a spoon to stir, then kneading by hand as the batter becomes a dough. Knead well until the dough feels elastic, then shape it into a ball with well-floured hands, put it on a greased baking tray, cover with a damp cloth and stand in a warm place until doubled in size.

Turn the risen dough onto a floured board and divide in half or in quarters. Flour and flatten each piece and then roll up like a Swiss roll. Repeat two or three times with each piece. Put each roll in a greased loaf tin (450g (1 lb.) or 1kg (2 lb.) size) and press down well. Cover with a damp cloth and leave in a warm place until the dough rises to the top of the tins.

Brush over the tops with milk and bake in a hot oven 230°C (450°F, Gas Mark 8), for 10 minutes. Lower the oven to 200°C (400°F, Gas Mark 6) and cook small loaves for a further 20 minutes, large loaves 30-35 minutes. Turn onto wire racks to cool.

White Bread

1.3kg + 4 dessertspoons (3 lb.)
plain flour
150ml (¼ pint) boiling milk
mixed with 700ml (1¼
pints) cold water
4 level teaspoons salt
50g (2 oz) fresh yeast or 2
teaspoons dried
1 level teaspoon brown sugar
1 teaspoon syrup or honey
(optional)

Sieve the flour into a warm basin and set aside in a warm place. Divide the milk and water mixture into two bowls; dissolve the salt in one and whisk the yeast in the other. Add the sugar, and syrup or honey if used, to the yeast mixture. Now mix the two liquids together and pour into a well in the centre of the flour, mixing with the hands.

Turn onto a floured board and knead well for 10 minutes until the dough is smooth. Put it back in the warm basin, cover with a warm damp cloth and stand in a warm place until doubled in size.

Turn onto a floured board again, knead lightly, then divide in half or in quarters (1kg (2 lb.) or 450g (1 lb.) loaves). Mould each piece to fit a well-greased tin, cover again with a damp cloth and set in a warm place until the dough fills the tins.

Brush over the tops with milk and bake in a hot oven, 260°C (500°F, Gas Mark 9), for the first 10 minutes, then at 200°C (400°F, Gas Mark 6) for a further 20 minutes before opening the oven door. The 450g (1 lb.) loaves will be done in this time, larger ones will take up to 45 minutes. (Test the loaves by turning them out of the tins and tapping the base—if they sound hollow they are ready. If not, return to the oven for another 5–10 minutes.) Cool on wire racks.

Special Breads

Apple Bread

A very light, pleasant bread can be made using a mixture of apples and flour in the proportions of 450g (1 lb.) apples to 900g (2lb.) flour. The standard quantity of yeast is used as in ordinary bread, 50g (2 oz) yeast to 1.8kg (4 lb.) flour, and is mixed with the flour and warm pulp of cooked apples. (Very little water is needed—none, generally, if the apples are very fresh.)

The dough is allowed to rise for 3 to 4 hours and then turned into three well-greased 450g (1 lb.) tins, and baked in a moderate oven, 190°C (375°F, Gas Mark 5), for 1-1¼ hours. Cool on a wire rack.

Lardy Cake

white bread dough using 900g
(2 lb.) flour (see page 107)
350g (¾ lb.) lard
350g (¾ lb.) granulated sugar
350g (¾ lb.) mixed dried fruit
50g (2 oz) cut peel

After the first proving, roll out the dough to an oblong and spread with half the fat, sugar, fruit and peel. Then fold in three as for flaky pastry. Roll and turn the dough, repeat with the remainder of the ingredients and roll again.

Shape the dough to fit three 450g (1 lb.) baking tins, score across the top with a sharp knife and sprinkle with a little sugar. Prove again, put the dough in the greased tins and bake at 220°C (425°F, Gas Mark 7) for 45 minutes.

Serve hot or cold.

Yeast Buns

Baps

450g (1 lb.) plain flour
50g + ½ dessertspoon (2 oz)
lard
1 level teaspoon granulated
sugar
25g (1 oz) yeast
150ml (¼ pint) each of
lukewarm milk and water
2 level teaspoons salt

Sieve the flour, rub in the lard and add the sugar.

Whisk the yeast in half the liquid and dissolve the salt in the remainder. Mix both liquids into the flour to make a dough, then set aside in a warm place to prove.

Knead well, then divide the dough into circular rolls about 10 cm (4 inches) in diameter. Put the baps on a greased baking tray, prove again, brush over the tops with milk and then bake at 230°C (450°F, Gas Mark 8) for 20 minutes. Cool on a wire rack.

about 12 baps

Bath Buns

225g (½ lb.) flour
½ teaspoon salt
100g + 1 dessertspoon (¼ lb.)
butter
50g + ½ dessertspoon (2 oz)
caster sugar
15g + ½ dessertspoon (½ oz)
yeast

Sieve together the flour and salt and rub in butter. Add three dessertspoons of the caster sugar.

Cream the yeast with the remaining caster sugar. Beat the eggs, add them to the milk and blend with the yeast. Pour this into a well in the flour and mix thoroughly to a soft dough. Set to rise in a warm place for 10–15 minutes.

Divide the risen dough into 8 portions, knead lightly and shape into buns. Fold a little crushed candied-peel sugar and candied

2 eggs
½ teacup lukewarm milk
25g (1 oz) candied peel
sugar from candied peel
4 sugar lumps, roughly
   crushed
a handful of currants

peel into the centre of each and place on a greased and floured baking tray.

Brush over with water and sprinkle with crushed lump sugar and a few currants. Set in a warm place to rise for 10-15 minutes, then bake in a hot oven, 230°C (450°F, Gas Mark 8), for about 10-20 minutes, depending whether the buns are large or small.

makes 8 large buns or 12 small

Hot Cross Buns

225g (½ lb.) flour
3 dessertspoons butter
25g (1 oz) granulated sugar
2 level teaspoons mixed spice
40g (1½ oz) mixed dried fruit
15g (½ oz) yeast
100 ml + 1 dessertspoon (4 fl.
   oz) lukewarm milk
½ level teaspoon salt
1 egg, beaten
beaten egg to brush over

Sieve the flour into a basin, rub in the butter and mix in the sugar, spice and dried fruit.

Whisk the yeast with half the milk, dissolve the salt in the remainder and add the egg. Pour the yeast mixture into a well in the centre of the flour, allow to stand for several minutes and then add the remaining liquid, mixing to a light consistency.

Knead, then prove in a warm place for about 30 minutes. Knead again and roll the dough out to about 2.5 cm (1 inch) thick. Divide into buns. Place them on a greased baking tray and prove again for about a further 30 minutes.

Brush over the tops with beaten egg and cut a cross on each bun with the back of a knife (in the West Country we do not usually add the cross in pastry). Bake at 230°C (425°F, Gas Mark 8) for about 25 minutes until golden and cooked through.

about 6 buns

Croissants

225g (½ lb.) flour
2 level teaspoons granulated
   sugar
15g (½ oz) yeast
150ml (¼ pint) lukewarm
   water
½ level teaspoon salt
75g + ½ dessertspoon (3 oz)
   butter
beaten egg to brush over

Croissants scarcely qualify as traditional West Country cooking, but they are such a delicious addition to any breakfast, and are so rarely home-made, that I include them here in the hope that more people may try what is a much simpler recipe than is generally imagined.

Sieve the flour into a warm basin, make a well in the centre and add the sugar.

Whisk the yeast in half the water, dissolve the salt in the remainder and add the liquid to the well in the flour. Mix thoroughly to a dough, then set aside in a warm place for about 20 minutes until it has risen by nearly half as much again.

Make the butter into a neat parcel with your fingers, flatten the dough and put the butter in the centre, folding it up all round. Roll and fold as for puff pastry.

Set the dough aside in a cool place for 30 minutes, then roll and fold again two or three times. Roll out to 3mm (⅛ inch) thick, cut into 10-cm (4-inch) wide strips and then into triangles (Diagram 1). Roll each triangle up towards the point (Diagram 2), then curve into a horseshoe (Diagram 3).

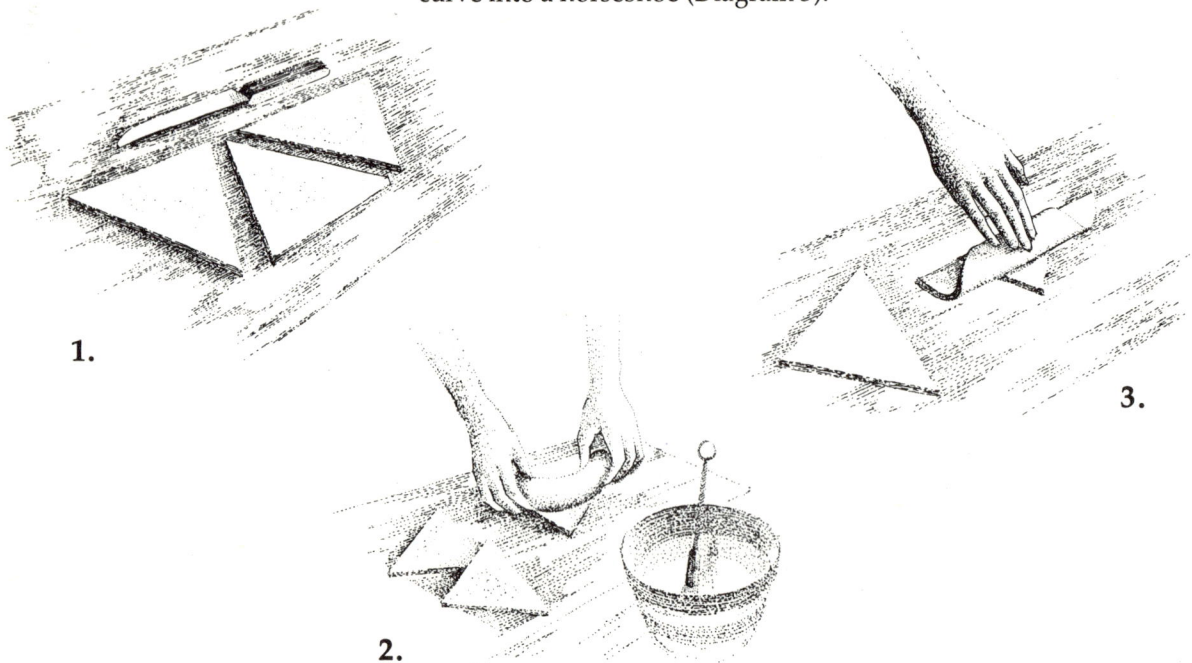

1.

3.

2.

Prove again on a greased baking tray. Brush with beaten egg and bake in a hot oven 230°C (450°F, Gas Mark 8), for about 30 minutes until golden brown.

Serve at once; or allow to cool on a wire rack, store in an airtight container and reheat until hot through before serving.

about 6 croissants

Sally Lunns

225g (½ lb.) flour
50g + ½ dessertspoon (2 oz) butter
15g (½ oz) yeast
½ level teaspoon granulated sugar
150ml (¼ pint) lukewarm milk
1 egg
½ level teaspoon salt

Sieve the flour into a basin, rub in the butter and set aside in a warm place.

Mix the yeast with the sugar and whisk with a little of the milk, then pour into a well in the centre of the flour. Cover the yeast with flour and replace the basin in a warm place while the yeast soaks in.

Add the egg and the remaining milk in which the salt has been dissolved, to the dough and beat well. Turn into a warm, 23-cm (9-inch), greased round cake tin, mark out the segments and cook for 20 minutes at 190°C (375°F, Gas Mark 5). Eat hot or cold. (Traditionally the Sally Lunn was baked in one large round and then broken in pieces when it was cooked.)

Double Bakes

675g + 1 dessertspoon (1½ lb.)
  plain flour
100g + 1 dessertspoon (¼ lb.)
  butter
50g + ½ dessertspoon (2 oz)
  lard or dripping
15g (½ oz) yeast
425ml (¾ pint) equal
  quantities lukewarm milk
  and water
1 level teaspoon salt

Sieve the flour into a basin and rub in the butter and lard. Whisk the yeast in half the liquid, dissolve the salt in the remainder and add both to a well in the centre of the flour. Mix to a dough.

Prove for about half an hour, then roll out to 1 cm (½ inch) thick and cut in rounds. Put on a greased baking tray and prove again for a further 30 minutes, then bake at 230°C (450°F, Gas Mark 8) for about 15 minutes until golden.

Remove from the oven, split across the centre, then bake again until hard—about a further 15 minutes.

about 18 double bakes

Scones and 'small breads'

Cheese Scones

200g (7 oz) flour
2 teaspoons baking powder
50g + ½ dessertspoon (2 oz)
  butter
50 g + ½ dessertspoon (2 oz)
  Cheddar cheese, grated
a pinch of black pepper
150ml (¼ pint) milk

Sieve the flour and baking powder into a basin, then rub in the butter. Add the cheese and pepper, and mix well to a stiff dough with the milk.

Roll out on a floured board and cut into rounds. Put on a greased baking tray and cook at 230°C (450°F, Gas Mark 8) for 20 minutes.

6 – 7 small scones

Cornish Hot Cakes

225g (½ lb.) freshly boiled
  potatoes
50g + ½ dessertspoon (2 oz)
  chopped suet
100g + 2 dessertspoon (¼ lb.)
  flour
1 teaspoon baking powder
50 g + ½ dessertspoon (2 oz)
  sultanas
1 egg, beaten

Sieve the potatoes into a basin while still hot and add the suet. Sieve the flour with the baking powder and stir them into the potatoes. Add the sultanas, mix well and bind to a firm dough with the egg.

Roll out and cut into rounds. Place on a baking tray, brush over with milk and cook in a moderate oven, 180°C (350°F, Gas Mark 4), for about 25 minutes.

about 16 – 18 cakes

Chudleighs

(Cut Rounds, Splits, Tuff Cakes)

900g (2 lb.) flour
a pinch of salt
2 teaspoons baking powder
1 tablespoon caster sugar
3 dessertspoons butter
milk and water to mix

There is an interesting historical point to be found one day as to why the different names obtain for what is practically the same thing: chudleighs do not, as far as I know, originate in Chudley; tuff cakes are probably turf cakes from the turf fires of Cornwall; but splits and cut rounds? I haven't yet been able to find out the reason for these names but perhaps one day I shall.

Sieve the flour, salt, baking powder and sugar into a basin. Rub in the butter and then mix to a firm paste with equal parts of milk and water.

Roll out to about 1 cm (½ inch) thick, cut into rounds, put on a baking tray and cook in a fairly hot oven, 220°C (425°F, Gas Mark 7), for about a quarter of an hour.

Cool on wire racks and serve cold.

about 18-20

Cornish Splits

15g (½ oz) fresh yeast
1 dessertspoon caster sugar
275ml + 2 teaspoons (½ pint) tepid milk
450g (1 lb.) flour
¼ teaspoon salt
25g (1 oz) butter

Cream the yeast and sugar together until they are liquid, then add the milk.

Sieve the flour and salt into a basin. Meanwhile, melt the butter very gently and pour it and the milk into a well in the centre of the flour. Mix to a smooth dough, then set aside in a warm place for 45 minutes.

Shape the dough into small round cakes and put them on a floured baking tray. Cook in a hot oven, 220°C (425°F, Gas Mark 7), for 15 – 20 minutes.

To eat hot, split through the centre, spread with butter and serve at once. Or they may be left until cold, then split and buttered, or eaten with cream, jam or treacle. Splits eaten with cream and treacle are known as 'thunder and lightning'.

about 12 splits

Wholemeal Scones

225g (½ lb.) wholemeal flour
1 teaspoon baking powder
¼ teaspoon salt
50-75g (2-3 oz) butter
milk to mix

Mix the flour, baking powder and salt in a basin and rub in the butter. Mix with sufficient milk to give a soft dough, then turn onto a floured board, roll out and cut into rounds. Put on a greased baking tray, brush over with milk and cook in a hot oven, 230°C (450°F, Gas Mark 8), for 10 – 15 minutes.

about 6 scones

Devonshire 'Tetti Cakes'

225g (½ lb.) flour
¼ teaspoon salt
150g + 1½ dessertspoons
  6 oz) dripping or butter
50g + ½ dessertspoon (2 oz)
  granulated sugar
50 g + ½ dessertspoon (2 oz)
  currants
1 egg, beaten

These are the Devonshire version of Cornish Hot Cakes (page 113).

Sieve the flour and salt into a basin. Rub in the fat well, then add the sugar, currants and egg, mixing thoroughly.

Roll out on a floured surface to about 1-cm (½-inch) thickness. Cut into rounds. Either put the cakes on a greased baking tray and cook in the oven at 180°C (350°F, Gas Mark 4) for 25 minutes, or fry them until golden on each side.

Serve hot, split through the centre and buttered.

makes 18-20 small cakes

Drop Scones

225g (½ lb.) flour
½ teaspoon bicarbonate of
  soda
½ teaspoon cream of tartar
50g + ½ dessertspoon (2 oz)
  granulated sugar
2 eggs, beaten
275ml + 2 teaspoons (½ pint)
  milk (approx.)

Sieve the flour, bicarbonate of soda and cream of tartar into a basin and add the sugar. Stir in the eggs and enough of the milk to make a batter.

Have ready either a girdle or a thick-bottomed frying pan, lightly greased and very hot. Drop spoonfuls of the mixture onto the surface and let them cook until bubbles rise, then turn with a knife and cook on the other side (they will take about 5 or 6 minutes in all). Have a clean tea cloth beside the stove and lay the cooked drop scones on it, covering them with another cloth—this prevents them from drying. Butter and serve hot.

about 6 scones

Potato Scones

150 g + 3 dessertspoons (6 oz)
  flour
2 teaspoons baking powder
50 g + ½ dessertspoon (2 oz)
  butter
75 g + ½ dessertspoon (3 oz)
  mashed potato
milk to mix

Sieve the flour and baking powder into a bowl and rub in the butter. Add the mashed potato and mix with enough milk to give a stiff dough.

Turn onto a floured board and roll out to about 2cm (¾ inch) thick. Cut into scones and cook on a greased baking tray at 230°C (450°F, Gas Mark 8) for 10– 12 minutes.

makes 4-5 scones

CAKES

Large Cakes

Baking Sheet Cake

450g (1 lb.) self-raising flour
a pinch of salt
½ teaspoon mixed spice
150g + 1½ dessertspoons
(6 oz) butter, lard or dripping
150g + 1½ dessertspoons
(6 oz) sugar
225g (½ lb.) dried mixed fruit
2 teaspoons chopped peel

Sieve the flour, salt and spice into a bowl and rub in the fat. Add the sugar, fruit and peel, mixing to a good dry dough. Form into a ball with your hands, put onto a greased baking tray and press out to a round about 5 cm (2 inches) thick. Sprinkle thickly with sugar and bake in a hot oven, 230°C (450°F, Gas Mark 8), for about 20 minutes.

To test, turn the cake out, tap the bottom and if it sounds hollow it is ready—if not, bake for another 5 minutes or so. Cool on a wire rack.

Date and Nut Cake

325g + 2 dessertspoons (¾ lb.)
flour
150g + 1½ dessertspoons (6 oz)
butter
150g + 1½ dessertspoons
6 oz) brown sugar
1 teaspoon ground cinnamon
150g + 1½ dessertspoons
6 oz) chopped dates
150g + 1½ dessertspoons
(6 oz) chopped mixed nuts
275ml + 2 teaspoons (½ pint)
apple purée
1 level teaspoon bicarbonate of
soda
1 tablespoon milk

topping

1 teaspoon chopped mixed nuts

1 teaspoon chopped dates

1 dessertspoon soft brown sugar

1 level teaspoon ground
cinnamon

Sieve the flour into a basin and rub in the butter. Mix in the sugar, cinnamon, dates and nuts, then make a well in the centre and add the apple purée.

Dissolve the bicarbonate of soda in the milk, add this to the well and thoroughly mix the ingredients.

Turn the mixture into a 1-kg (2-lb.) greased oblong bread tin and sprinkle over the topping of the nuts, dates, sugar and cinnamon mixed together. Bake in a moderate oven, 180°C (350°F, Gas Mark 4), for 1½ hours. Test by tapping the base of the cake, which should sound hollow. Cool on a wire rack.

Dripping Cake

450g (1 lb.) self-raising flour
1 teaspoon mixed spice
½ teaspoon grated nutmeg
a pinch of salt
150g + 1½ dessertspoons
  (6 oz) good clear dripping
275g + ½ dessertspoon (10 oz)
  soft brown sugar
325g + 1 dessertspoon (¾ lb.)
  mixed dried fruit
2 eggs, beaten
milk to mix

Sieve the flour, spice, nutmeg and salt into a bowl and rub in the dripping. Add the sugar and fruit, then the eggs and enough milk to give a good dropping consistency.

Turn into a 23-cm (9-inch) greased cake tin and bake in a moderate oven, 180°C (350°F, Gas Mark 4), for 1½-2 hours. Test by tapping the base of the cake which should sound hollow. Cool on a wire rack.

Kitchen Cake (or Sarah's Cake)

450g (1 lb.) self-raising flour
½ teaspoon ground mace
½ teaspoon ground nutmeg
325g + 1 dessertspoon (¾ lb.)
  butter
325g + 1 dessertspoon (¾ lb.)
  demerara sugar
100g + ½ dessertspoon (¼ lb.)
  chopped mixed peel
3 eggs beaten

Sieve the flour and spices into a bowl. Rub in the butter, then add the sugar and peel. Add the eggs and mix the ingredients thoroughly.

Bake in a 23-cm (9-inch) well-greased tin at 150°C (300°F, Gas Mark 2) for 1½-2 hours. Test by tapping the base of the cake which should sound hollow. Cool on a wire rack.

Plain Seed Cake

325g + 2 dessertspoons (¾ lb.)
  self-raising flour
a pinch of salt
150g + 1½ dessertspoons
  (6 oz) butter
150g + 1½ dessertspoons
  (6 oz) sugar
40g (1½ oz) caraway seeds
1 large egg, beaten
milk to mix

Sieve the flour and salt into a bowl and rub in the butter. Add the sugar and caraway seeds, then mix with the egg and enough milk to give a good dropping consistency.

Bake in a 20-cm (8-inch) greased cake tin in a moderate oven, 190°C (375°F, Gas Mark 5), for 1½ hours. Test by tapping the base of the cake which should sound hollow. Cool on a wire rack.

Soda Cake

225g (½ lb.) flour
a pinch of salt
½ teaspoon bicarbonate of
   soda
½ teaspoon cream of tartar
a pinch of grated nutmeg
125g + 1 dessertspoon (5 oz)
   butter
125g + 1 dessertspoon (5 oz)
   granulated sugar
150g + 1½ dessertspoons
   (6 oz) currants
1 egg, beaten
sour milk to mix (or add a small
   teaspoon lemon juice or a
   few drops of vinegar to 150
   ml (¼ pint) fresh milk and
   leave to stand overnight)

Sieve the flour, salt, bicarbonate of soda, cream of tartar and nutmeg into a basin. Rub in the butter, then add the sugar and currants. Mix with the egg and sufficient milk to give a dropping consistency.

Bake in an 18-cm (7-inch) greased cake tin in a moderate oven, 190°C (375°F, Gas Mark 5), for about an hour. Test by tapping the base of the cake which should sound hollow. Cool on a wire rack.

Somerset Farmhouse Cider Cake

100g + 1 dessertspoon (¼ lb.)
   butter
100g + 1 dessertspoon (¼ lb.)
   sugar
2 eggs
225g (½ lb.) flour
½ a nutmeg, grated, or 1
   teaspoon powdered nutmeg
1 teaspoon bicarbonate of soda
1 teacup still cider

One of the great advantages of this recipe is that the cake will keep for a month or more.

Beat the butter and sugar to a cream and then beat in the eggs one at a time. Sieve the flour, nutmeg and bicarbonate of soda into a separate bowl, then stir half the flour into the butter mixture.

Beat the cider to a froth and pour over this mixture. Stir in the remaining flour and mix everything thoroughly.

Bake in an 18-cm (7-inch) greased cake tin in a moderate oven, 190°C (375°F, Gas Mark 5), for about an hour. Test by tapping the base of the cake which should sound hollow. Cool on a wire rack.

Vinegar Cake

450g (1 lb.) flour
100g (¼ lb.) butter
100g (¼ lb.) dripping
100g (¼ lb.) raisins

Sieve the flour into a bowl and rub in the fats, then stir in the raisins, currants and sugar.

Put the milk in a large jug and add the vinegar. Dissolve the bircarbonate of soda in a tablespoonful of additional milk, then

225g (½ lb.) currants
225g (½ lb.) soft brown sugar
150ml (¼ pint) milk
3 tablespoons vinegar
1 teaspoon bicarbonate of soda

pour this into the milk and vinegar, which will froth up and while still frothing must be stirred into the ingredients in the bowl.

Bake in a 23-cm (9-inch) well-greased cake tin in a moderate oven, 190°C (375°F, Gas Mark 5) for an hour. Test by tapping the base of the cake which should sound hollow. Cool on a wire rack.

Sultana Cake

325g + 2 dessertspoons (¾ lb.)
  self-raising flour
¼ teaspoon salt
150g + 1½ dessertspoons
  (6 oz) butter
150g + 1½ dessertspoons
  (6 oz) sultanas
150g + 1½ dessertspoons
  (6 oz) soft brown sugar
1 teaspoon grated lemon rind
1 egg, beaten
milk to mix

Sieve the flour and salt into a basin and rub in the butter. Add the sultanas, sugar and lemon rind, then mix in the egg and enough milk to give a dropping consistency.

Bake in a 20-cm (8-inch) greased cake tin at 190°C (375°F, Gas Mark 5) for about an hour. Test by tapping the base of the cake which should sound hollow. Cool on a wire rack.

Small Cakes
Date Crunchies

225g (½ lb.) flour
100g + 2 dessertspoons (¼ lb.)
  rolled oats
75g + ½ dessertspoon (3 oz)
  soft brown sugar
125g + 1 dessertspoon (5 oz)
  butter
325g + 1 dessertspoon (¾ lb.)
  chopped dates
1 teaspoon grated lemon rind
2 tablespoons water

Sieve the flour into a bowl and add the oats and sugar. Meanwhile, melt the butter very gently, pour it over the dry ingredients and mix well.

Put the dates into a small pan with the lemon rind and water. Heat gently, stirring occasionally, until the mixture is soft (adding a little extra water if necessary).

Spread half the flour and oats mixture over the greased base of a Swiss roll tin, about 15 x 25cm (6 x 10 inches), cover with the date filling and finish with the rest of the flour and oats.

Bake in a moderate oven, 190°C (375°F, Gas Mark 5), for an hour—the mixture will begin to come away from the sides of the tin when the crunchies are ready. Cut into fingers, using the back of a knife, while still in the tin and still hot. Cool in the tin before lifting out onto a rack.

Dark Moist Gingerbread

150g + 1½dessertspoons
   (6 oz) lard
150g + 1½ dessertspoons
   (6 oz) soft brown sugar
150g + 1½ dessertspoons
   (6 oz) treacle
450g (1 lb.) flour
1 teaspoon ground ginger
1 teaspoon bicarbonate of soda
milk to mix

Melt the fat and sugar with the treacle in a large pan over gentle heat. Meanwhile, sieve the flour and ginger into a bowl and when the fat and sugar mixture is liquid, remove the pan from the heat and stir in the flour.

Dissolve the bicarbonate of soda in a little water, then mix it with half a cup of milk and pour into the other ingredients, adding sufficient extra milk and mixing thoroughly until a pouring consistency is obtained.

Bake in a 25 x 13-cm (10½ x 5¼-inch) greased tin in a slow oven, 150°C (300°F, Gas Mark 2), for two hours. Test by tapping the base which should sound hollow. Leave the gingerbread to cool in the tin, but mark out in squares with a sharp knife while still hot.

Fruit Gingerbread

550g (1¼ lb.) flour
35g (1¼ oz) ground ginger
1 tablespoon soft brown sugar
100g (¼ lb.) glacé cherries,
   halved
100g (¼ lb.) mixed peel
100g (¼ lb.) almonds
1 teaspoon bicarbonate of soda
150ml (¼ pint) milk
100g (¼ lb.) butter
450g (1 lb.) golden syrup
2 eggs

Sieve the flour and ginger into a basin and add the sugar, cherries, peel and almonds.

Dissolve the bicarbonate of soda in a little of the milk.

Melt the butter with the syrup. Beat the eggs, add them to the syrup and butter and mix these with the flour. Last of all add the milk and soda. Mix well and turn into a 26 x 13-cm (10½ x 5¼-inch) greased baking tin.

Bake in a slow oven, 150°C (300°F, Gas Mark 2), for about 1½ hours. Test by tapping the base which should sound hollow. Leave to cool in the tin but mark out in squares with a sharp knife while still hot.

Honey Bran Knobs

2 cups flour
1 teaspoon baking powder
1 teaspoon cinnamon
½ teaspoon salt
3 cups butter
½ cup soft brown sugar
½ cup honey
2 eggs, well beaten
¾ teaspoon bicarbonate of
   soda
2-3 cups milk

I believe that this old recipe crossed the Atlantic and then came back again to Plymouth by way of sailors. I give the original cup measurements as they are consistent throughout.

Sieve the flour, baking powder, cinnamon and salt into a small bowl. Meanwhile, melt the butter over gentle heat, pour it into a large bowl and add the sugar, honey and eggs, mixing thoroughly.

Dissolve the bicarbonate of soda in the milk, then add the sifted dry ingredients in alternating batches with the milk to the butter and egg mixture in the bowl. Stir in the raisins, nuts, bran and vanilla essence, mixing well.

½ cup raisins
½ cup chopped mixed nuts
2½ cups bran
a few drops of vanilla essence

Drop teaspoonfuls of the mixture onto a 15 x 25 (6 x 10-inch) well-greased baking tray and cook in a hot oven, 220°C (425°F, Gas Mark 7), for 10 minutes. Cool on a wire rack.

Honey Flapjacks

75g + ½ dessertspoon (3 oz) butter
75g + 1 dessertspoon (3 oz) soft brown sugar
1 tablespoon honey
150g + 3 dessertspoons (6 oz) rolled oats

Cream the butter and sugar until soft. Warm the honey (in a ladle over gentle heat) and beat it into the mixture. Work the oats in gradually. Spread the mixture to about 1-cm (½ inch) thickness in a 15 x 25-cm (6 x 10-inch) well-greased, shallow tin and bake in a moderate oven 190°C (375°F, Gas Mark 5), for 40 minutes.

Allow to cool in the tin, then cut into fingers, and only remove from the tin when the flapjacks are quite cold.

Plain Shortbread

150g + 3 dessertspoons (6 oz) flour
50g + ½ dessertspoon (2 oz) caster sugar
100g + 1 dessertspoon (¼ lb.) butter

Sieve the flour and sugar into a bowl and knead in the butter. When the mixture binds, press it into a 15-cm (6-inch) round cake tin. Prick over the top with a fork and crimp the edges between finger and thumb.

Bake in a moderate oven, 180°C (350°F, Gas Mark 4), for about 30 minutes until firm and just golden. Leave the shortbread in the tin until it is just cool, then lift out onto a wire rack and dredge with caster sugar. When completely cold, cut in wedges.

(For other shortbread recipes see under Butter, Cream and Cheese, page 42)

Rich Shortbread

225g (½ lb.) flour
225g (½ lb.) rice flour
225g (½ lb.) butter
100g + 1 dessertspoon (¼ lb.) caster sugar
1 egg, lightly beaten
a little cream or rich milk to mix

Sieve together the flours, then rub in the butter. Mix in the sugar, the egg and just enough cream to make a stiff dough. Knead until the mixture is smooth, then roll cut to about 1-cm (½-inch) thick on a floured board and cut into fingers or other shapes. Put on a 15 x 25-cm (6 x 10-inch) buttered tray and bake in a slow oven, 120°C (250°F, Gas Mark ½), for about 20 minutes until just golden.

Dredge with caster sugar while still hot and transfer to a wire rack to cool.

BISCUITS

Almond Biscuits

50g + 1 dessertspoon (2 oz) flour
50g + ½ dessertspoon (2 oz) caster sugar
50g + 1 dessertspoon (2 oz) ground almonds
50g + ½ dessertspoon (2 oz) butter
1 egg, beaten

Sieve the flour and mix with the sugar and almonds. Rub in the butter and then bind to a stiff dough using as much as is necessary of the egg. Roll out to about ½ cm (¼ inch) thick and cut in rounds. Bake in a moderate oven, 190°C (375°F, Gas Mark 5), for about 15 minutes. Cool on a wire rack before storing in an airtight container.

makes 20 small biscuits

Butter Wafers

50g + ½ dessertspoon (2 oz) caster sugar
25g (1 oz) flour
25g (1 oz) flaked almonds
white of an egg
25g (1 oz) butter

Mix together the sugar, sifted flour and almonds, then stir in the unbeaten egg white.

Meanwhile melt the butter very gently, taking care not to let it brown. Gently fold the butter into the mixture. Drop dessertspoons of the mixture onto a 15 x 25-cm (6 x 10-inch) greased tray and bake at 190°C (375°F, Gas Mark 5) for 5-7 minutes. Lift the wafers off gently with a palette knife and put them over a rolling pin or a bottle so that they curl as they cool. Store in an airtight container, where they will keep for several weeks.

about 12 – 14 biscuits

Digestive Biscuits

100g + 2 dessertspoons (¼ lb.) wholemeal flour
100g + 2 dessertspoons (¼ lb.) medium oatmeal
75g + ½ dessertspoon (3 oz) butter
3 dessertspoons caster sugar
a pinch of salt
¼ teaspoon bicarbonate of soda
half a beaten egg

Sieve the flour into a bowl, add the oatmeal and then rub in the butter. Stir in the sugar, salt and bicarbonate of soda and bind the mixture with the egg.

Turn onto a floured board, roll out to 2 cm (¾ inch) thick, sprinkle lightly with oatmeal and press the rolling pin gently over the top. Cut into shapes and bake on a 20 x 25-cm (8 x 10-inch) greased tin at 180°C (350°F, Gas Mark 4) for about 15 minutes.

makes about 24 small biscuits

Wholemeal biscuits

225g (½ lb.) wholemeal flour
100g + 2 dessertspoons (¼ lb.)
   plain flour
a pinch of salt
¼ teaspoon mixed spice
25g (1 oz) butter
25g (1 oz) soft brown sugar
milk to mix

Sieve together the flours, salt and spice and rub in the butter. Mix in the sugar and enough milk to give a stiff dough. Knead well, then roll out thinly and prick all over with a fork. Cut into rounds with a large cutter and bake on a 20 x 25-cm (8 x 10-inch) greased tin in a moderate oven, 190°C (375°F, Gas Mark 5), for about 15 minutes. Cool on a wire rack.

makes about 12 large biscuits

Cheese Snips

shortcrust pastry
beaten egg
100 g (¼ lb.) strong cheese,
   grated, per 450g (1 lb.)
   of pastry

This is a good way to use up odd bits of pastry left over from other dishes.

Roll out the pastry, brush over with beaten egg, sprinkle on the cheese and bake on a greased tin in a hot oven, 230°C (450°F, Gas Mark 8), until the cheese is crisp. Serve hot.

Drinks
of the West

Drinks of the West

To visitors, the south-west probably spells 'zider' and more 'zider', but we do have other drinks as well: mead, for instance, made from 'honey and water boyled together if it be fyned and pure it preserveth helth'; and perry, being the fermented juice of the pear, as cider is the product of the apple.

Beer is not a speciality of our region, though one of the last remaining independent breweries still maintains, in Dorset, its reputation for good beer. Not being a beer drinker myself I am no judge of the merits of bottled versus 'real ale', but I do know that the big combines have in general forced out the traditionally brewed beers, substituting—as also with cider—a frothy carbonated drink which is served in every public house. Big business always seems to mean this sort of result; their very nature demands vast distribution areas and huge processing plants, and the regulations tend to be on their side so that small concerns have to tag along as best they can.

Home-made wines are so much a product of the individual local maker that they cannot really come within the scope of this book, but I am grateful to be able to include here a section on English wines by Pamela Vandyke Price, Wine Correspondent of *The Times*:

> There is nothing either 'quaint' or comic about English wines; they have a proud tradition. From 1066 onwards the religious houses and many estates made wine, and only from 1914 until 1965 was there a gap in production. Vineyards making wine commercially today have benefitted from the most informed advice from the wine institutes of the world and, after all, climate is often more of a problem in Germany than in England, and hail and frost can destroy vines in France. By now English wine-makers know more about their particular vineyards, their wines have matured, the vineyards themselves have grown up and wine-making methods have been adapted to make excellent white wines. The huge wave of chalk that makes the Champagne vineyard curls under the Channel to emerge as the foundation of many southern English vineyards.
>
> Our wines often make use of classic wine grapes, and sometimes these yield an even higher quality than in better-known wine areas. We make elegant, pleasing whites, some with vigour and charm, many of which are now able to bear favourable comparison with certain German, Luxemburg and French wines, price for price. I see no reason why those that are pretty good should not, in time, become even better. They

can be delicious, interesting aperitifs; good with our shellfish, from prawns to winkles and cockles; agreeable with cold chicken, cold roast of lamb or veal; enhancing to fish fingers, chicken pie, patties or rissoles; or simply as any-time refreshment—and there are now plenty of eminent members of the wine trade who will agree about the quality of English wines.

Some vineyards in the south-west are producing wine of a very high quality. Visitors can discover this for themselves by being conducted over these establishments by the owners and buying the product of the vines. Details of the vineyards can be found in the directory on page 137.

So we come back to cider, the production of which has largely been taken over by the large combines whose touch, many people feel, has been the touch of death. As the campaigners for 'real ale' have revolted against the brewers who, apparently, had turned the national drink into a carbonated fizz, so perhaps the makers of cider will begin to accept the fact that we do not all want a sweet, gassy substitute which does not bear any relation to farmhouse cider.

When we first came to Devon we had two orchards of cider apples and these we let drop as directed, then gathered them up and took them to a neighbour's press to be made into cider. The result was a lesson to us. We were told when the big barrel was filled that 'sweet' cider could be drawn off and drunk at once, so draw it I did, the jugful going down most 'suently', (sweetly) as our young farmhand described it. I had been warned that it could 'fetch the legs from under a man', but surely they didn't mean that lovely smooth apple-orchard smelling drink? But they did, and some builders who were working for us found out the hard way too.

It's traditional in Devon, if there is a cask of cider in the barn, to allow delivery drivers and any workmen on the premises to draw off a jugful for their 'bate-time' (dinner hour) and the gang working for us building our new dairy were told they could do just that. But what we did not know was they were foreigners and, like me, they did not understand cider. I saw them draw a jugful to drink with their packed dinner, then I went out, and as it happened none of the rest of the family had any cause to go to that particular building again until it was knocking-off time.

I had vaguely wondered at the lack of the usual building noises coming from the dairy but it was only when the firm's driver turned up to take the men home that we saw what had happened. He peered over the half door of the barn in which they had been taking their meals, and then I saw him grin . . . he was a local man. He came over to me in the farmhouse, 'Come and have a look,' he said, so I went with him and looked over the door myself. There stretched out on the straw bales were the four men utterly dead to the world. They too had found that sweet cider went down very 'suently', and though they were none of them sure how much they had drunk they assured me that it wasn't much, 'us felt all right, see, Missus, till us came to get up, then it took us in our legs. Fancy mild-tasting stuff like that doing that to your legs.'

Few small cider-making enterprises exist now in the south-west. Farmers who used to make it for themselves and sell a little to their friends no longer do so, and the cider-apple orchards have been grubbed with the help of government grants. Government grants don't take any account of the magic of old names but I see that even scientific writers enjoy listing some of the varieties; after all, who could resist Hangdowns, Skyrm's Kerne, Old Foxwhelp, Slack-me-girdle, Golden Ball, Handsome Maud's, Ruby Streak, Yellow Styres, Golden Pippins, Woodbines Duckbill, Cats Heads, Sheeps' Noses and Lady's Finger?

I found in an old agricultural journal this description of how cider was made on one farm:

> It was a small mill belonging to a small farm, the mill was an old stone trough, with a wide splayed wooden rim, the heavy stone crusher rolled round pivoted on a worn oak beam. The press was a plain stone screw press standing in a stone trough. In autumn the apples were gathered in piles, and left to brown, the old pony was then fetched up and harnessed, then all the things which had been left from the year before were cleared out and the trough and press scoured out, then the woodwork was soaked in spring water. The apples were shovelled in and stirred with a wooden shovel, the pomace was then made the pony going round meanwhile. When the trough was full of crushed pulp this was collected into one of the pressing mats, these were folded over the pulp like a well made parcel and the mass was put on the stone base of the press. The screw was set on and the juice then ran swiftly down into the trough underneath. As this filled it was baled into the casks.

The Cornish miners would run a sheep's blood into the cask but in Devon they added milk and cream! Obviously no commercial cider could boast such additions.

Nothing like the same folklore seems to have built up over the making of perry, probably because most farms have a cider-apple orchard but few have any number of pear trees. I have a very old pear tree in my garden which every year is a mass of blossom and then, come the autumn, it bears a vast quantity of small, hard, totally inedible pears. Can it be a variety suitable for perry, I wonder? I should love to have a tree called Hendre Huffcap,

Turner's Barn or Merry Legs. Little or no perry is for sale on the open market, and the nearest most of us will get to it is by opening a bottle of that well-known party drink which carries on its label the figure of a small perky little animal, species unknown, with long legs and blue bow round its neck.

Mead is still made in the West Country by the monks of Buckfast Abbey but, alas, it is no longer on sale; it has no general popularity I think. Cider will always be the drink of this region, and in some cases its curse. They still tell the tale in this village of the farm labourer who would down half a gallon at a local pub and then faced with a three mile walk home before he got his Sunday dinner, would put a filled quart bottle into each pocket and so made his way home, with fairly frequent stops for refreshment as he went. 'Us always had to go and look for 'ee', his daughter told me. 'Us'd find him in the ditch more times than not.'

And to end this chapter with a real Cornish speciality, Kiddley Broth, which I had always imagined was a corruption of something to do with kidneys. Not a bit of it; here is how Claude Berry, in his delightful *Portrait of Cornwall*, describes his grandmother's making of it:

There is nothing Cornish about the word 'kiddley' here; though Kiddle Rock, at Padstow, off which are the good mussel beds, is probably a corruption of Guidal (the tide-net) Rock. 'Kiddley' comes from kettle, which we call kiddle, and kiddley broth is made by pouring boiling water upon pieces of bread which have been put into a basin, with pepper, salt, and a tiny lump of butter as seasoning. The broth is tasty, and had long been in Cornwall a stay-stomach of the poor—we often had it for breakfast—and a light meal for those recovering from an illness.

Eel Stew

450g (1 lb.) eels, skinned and
    cleaned
2 spring onions
1 garlic clove
parsley sprigs
2 bay leaves
salt
black pepper
water
150ml (¼ pint) still cider
4 – 6 small carrots, peeled and
    diced
100g (¼ lb.) mushrooms,
    sliced
1 tablespon butter

Cut the eels into 5-7½-cm (2-3 inch) long pieces and put them in a pan with the onions, garlic, parsley, bay leaves and seasoning. Add enough water to cover. Bring slowly to the boil, add the cider and simmer for 10-12 minutes.

Meanwhile, sauté the carrots and mushrooms in the butter until they are just tender. Keep warm.

Lift the eel from the liquor, arrange in a serving dish with the vegetables round about and keep warm. Strain the liquor through a sieve, return it to the pan and boil fast until it is reduced by about half. Pour this over the fish and vegetables and serve at once.

serves 2

Baked Shrimps

1 cup fresh white breadcrumbs
50g (2 oz) butter, melted
1 small onion, chopped
1 tablespoon chopped parsley
a pinch each of thyme,
    tarragon, nutmeg and mace
¼ teaspoon salt
black pepper
150ml (¼ pint) still cider
    (approx.)
1 garlic clove
approx. 1 litre (2 pints) peeled
    shrimps
1 cup fried breadcrumbs

Mix together the fresh breadcrumbs, butter, onion, parsley, herbs and seasoning. Pour on enough cider to thoroughly moisten the mixture.

Rub the cut garlic clove over a 1-litre (2-pint) fireproof dish and put alternate layers of herb mixture and shrimps into the dish, topping the final layer with the fried crumbs.

Bake in a moderate oven, 190°C (375°F, Gas Mark 5), for 20 – 25 minutes.

serves 4

Sole St Columb

2 sole
3 cups still dry cider
3 cups water
50g (2 oz) butter
50g (2 oz) flour
salt
black pepper
1 teaspoon lemon juice

Put the sole in a large saucepan with the cider and water and poach gently for about 10 minutes until cooked. Drain the fish and keep warm in a covered flameproof dish.

Reduce the poaching liquor to about half by boiling rapidly. Meanwhile, in a separate pan make a roux with the butter and flour. Add the liquid slowly, stirring constantly, then simmer for about 10 minutes. Season to taste and add the lemon juice.

Pour the sauce over the sole, brown lightly under the grill and serve at once.

serves 2

Stuffed Fillets of Plaice

2 fillets of
plaice per
person
575ml (1 pint)
still dry cider
per person

stuffing (for
each serving)
50g (2 oz)
mushrooms
cooked in
butter

25g (1 oz)
cooked rice
1 teaspoon
chopped
parsley
salt
black pepper
1 egg yolk,
beaten

Mix together the stuffing ingredients, binding with the egg yolk. Roll up each fillet round half the given quantity of stuffing and tie securely.

Lay the fish in a 1-litre (2-pint) buttered fireproof dish, pour on the cider, cover and bake for about 20 minutes at 180°C (350°F, Gas Mark 4).

Bacon in Cider

1kg (2 lb.) piece of collar bacon
575ml (1 pint) still cider
1 bouquet garni
50g (2 oz) brown sugar
1 teacup brown breadcrumbs,
toasted
12 cloves

Soak the bacon overnight in cold water. Drain it, put it into a saucepan with the cider and bouquet garni and simmer, allowing 20 minutes per 450g (1 lb.), plus an additional 20 minutes.

Drain off the cooking liquor, let the bacon cool and then remove the skin. Mix the sugar and breadcrumbs together and spread them over the fat on the bacon, then stick in the cloves to form a diamond pattern.

Cook the bacon in a fairly hot oven, 200°C (400°F, Gas Mark 6), for about 20 minutes until it is just golden. Seve hot or cold.

serves 4 – 5

Bacon with Cabbage

1kg (2 lb.) cabbage
6 peppercorns
6 cloves
2 medium onions, sliced
1kg (2 lb.) piece of bacon
1.1 litres (2 pints) still dry cider
50g (2 oz) soft brown sugar

Chop the cabbage roughly and put it in a deep saucepan with the peppercorns, cloves and onions. Put the bacon on top of the cabbage, pour on the cider and sprinkle the sugar over the bacon.

Bring to the boil, then reduce to a simmer, allowing 25 minutes per 450g (1 lb.) of bacon plus an extra 25 minutes. Just before serving, sprinkle a little more sugar over the bacon.

serves 6

Baked Pork Chops

1 loin chop per person
a little butter
1 onion per 2 chops
a pinch of marjoram
a pinch of basil
paprika
salt
pepper
still dry cider
water

Brown the chops in butter in a flameproof casserole over a moderate heat, then add the chopped onion, marjoram, basil, a dusting of paprika, salt, pepper and enough of an equal mixture of water and cider to keep the chops moist but not to cover them. Cover the casserole and bake in a moderate oven, 190°C (375°F, Gas Mark 5), for about an hour.

Savoury Stuffed Potatoes

4 large potatoes
50g (2 oz) butter
100g (¼ lb.) Cheddar cheese grated
4 teaspoons still dry cider
black pepper

Scrub the potatoes, prick the skins with a fork and bake in a moderate oven, 190°C (375°F, Gas Mark 5), for 1-1½ hours until cooked. Slice off the top of each potato and scoop out the contents into a bowl. Mash this potato with the butter, cheese, cider and seasoning until thoroughly creamy. Stuff the skins with this mixture and then bake for a further 10-15 minutes. Serve very hot.

serves 4

Spicy Potatoes

1kg (2 lb.) potatoes
25g (1 oz) butter
salt
black pepper
575ml (1 pint) still cider
50g (2 oz) Cheddar cheese, granted
1 tablespon chopped parsley

Peel the potatoes and slice them about 6mm (¼ inch) thick. Fill a 1-litre (2-pint) fireproof dish with layers of potato, dotting with butter and adding seasoning between each layer. Pour on enough cider to come almost to the top of the potatoes. Sprinkle the cheese and parsley over the top and dot with more butter.

Bake in a moderate oven, 190°C (375°F, Gas Mark 5), for at least an hour until the potatoes are tender and the top brown.

serves 4

Somerset Chicken Casserole

1½ – 1¾ kg (3½ – 4 lb.)
   roasting chicken, jointed
50g (2 oz) butter
2 medium onions, chopped
3 rashers of bacon, diced
1 garlic clove, crushed
2 tablespoons tomato purée
150ml (¼ pint) stock
150ml (¼ pint) still dry cider
salt
black pepper

In a large, heavy pan, brown the chicken joints in the butter. Add the onion and bacon, cook gently for 5 minutes, then add the garlic and cook slowly for a further 10 minutes.

Meanwhile, mix together the tomato purée, stock, cider and seasoning. Pour this over the chicken (add a little more cider if necessary so that the chicken is just covered), cover the pan and cook very slowly for 1½ hours. Serve the chicken with the liquor in which it was cooked as gravy.

serves 6 – 8

Stuffed Apples

1 cooking apple per person
1 large teaspoon mincemeat per
   apple
butter
1 tablespoon still dry cider per
   apple

Peel and core the apples and stand them in a fireproof dish. Fill each with mincemeat, dot butter on top and pour over the cider.

Bake in a moderate oven, 190°C (375°F, Gas Mark 5), basting occasionally, for about 30 minutes until the apples are tender but not bursting their skins. Serve hot or cold.

Cider Cream

275ml (¼ pint) double cream
2 tablespoons still cider
50g (2 oz) caster sugar
1 egg, beaten

This is a rich sauce for fruit puddings and sweet pies.

Whip the cream until stiff, then whip in the cider. Beat the sugar into the egg. Mix the cream and egg together and beat again.

This cream will keep in a refrigerator for up to 14 days.

Taunton Cake

150g + 1½ dessertspoons (6 oz)
   butter
150g + 1½ dessertspoons (6 oz)
   soft brown sugar
150g + 3 dessertspoons (6 oz)
   self-raising flour
3 eggs, beaten
2 tablespoons sweet cider

icing
100g (¼ lb.) icing sugar
still sweet cider to moisten
knob of butter
1 teaspoon honey

Somerset people eat this as a pudding rather than a cake.

Beat the butter and sugar together, then add, gradually and *alternately*, beating constantly, the sifted flour and the eggs. Stir in the cider. Turn into a 20-cm (8-inch) greased cake tin and bake in a fairly slow oven, 160°C (325°F, Gas Mark 3) for about an hour, or until a skewer comes out clean.

To make the icing: sift the icing sugar into a basin and set it over a saucepan of hot water. Stir in enough cider to moisten to a paste. Stir in the butter and honey and when they have just melted, pour the icing over the warm cake.

Devonshire Oranges

4 oranges
1 cup still sweet cider
75g (3 oz) granulated sugar
½ cup water

Peel and quarter the oranges and remove all the pips and pith. Arrange the quarters in a serving dish and pour over the cider.

Make a syrup by dissolving the sugar in the water over gentle heat and then bring to the boil, stirring frequently. When the syrup is just thickening, pour it over the oranges. Chill well before serving.

serves 4

Eggy'ot

2 eggs
2 tablespoons granulated sugar
1.1 litre (1 quart) hot beer

This drink seems to have originated with one which was given to nursing mothers and which contained milk rather than beer. I suspect the men added the alcoholic content to suit themselves. Beat the eggs with the sugar, pour over the hot beer and stir briskly.

Cider Punch

2¼ litre (2 quarts) still cider
½ litre (1¾ pints) gin or vodka
¼ litre (1¾ pints) sherry
2 oranges, with peel
1 lemon, with peel
3 tablespoons granulated sugar
3 sprigs fresh mint
1 syphon soda

Mix the cider with the gin or vodka and the sherry. Wash and slice the oranges and lemon and add them to the cider mixture with the sugar and crushed mint. Chill well.

Just before serving add soda according to taste. The punch can be served with ice or just as it is.

Makes about 20 glasses

Sampson

2 eggs
2 tablespoons granulated sugar
1.1 litres (1 quart) still hot cider

An old Cornish drink which is an excellent palliative for a cold.

Beat the eggs with the sugar, pour over the hot cider and stir briskly.

West Country Directory

A West Country directory of retailers of home-grown and home-made foods

Crusty or home-baked bread

Cornwall

Headon – Bude & Holsworthy

Devon

Bideford – Devon Creameries
Hemyock – Saunders
Honiton – North
Tiverton – Boundy

Dorset

Blandford Forum – Wrigglesworth
Wool at Wareham – Williams

Somerset

Bath – Old Red House Bakery
   (makers of the original Bath bun)
Dulverton – Balsoms

Biscuits

Cornwall

Truro – Furniss make a whole range of biscuits all under the name of 'Cornish Fairings'. These delicious biscuits are sold in tins, each containing one variety which is specified on the tin. They can be found in shops all over the south-west

Dorset

Morecombelake – Moores. Their Dorset Knobs are still being made and the firm has now added several varieties of biscuits to its range. The small factory can be visited and all products purchased there. Their biscuits are also sold in good delicatessens throughout the region

Dairy produce

Devon

Newton St Cures – J.G. Quicke & Partners sell traditionally made farmhouse cheese at their farm shop. Also farmhouse butter, cream, lactic cheese and real dairy ice-cream without artificial flavouring or colouring

Dorset

Beaminster (Blackdown) – Childhay Manor make clotted cream, double cream, cottage cheese and yoghourt. They sell in *Bournemouth, Sidmouth* and *Bridgwater*

Somerset

Axminster market – Coombe Farm (A.S. Warren) sell from their stall butter, cheese and cream. Also at markets in *Blandford Forum, Bridgwater, Bridport, Chard, Sherborne, Taunton, Yeovil*. Their vans also sell home-made cakes and savouries, special recipe sausages, chickens, brown eggs and honey
Bridgwater – (depot and market stall) Cricket Malherbie Dairies make farmhouse butter, cheese and cream. Also depots at *Chard, Crewkerne, Yeovil* and their shops at *Bridport, Williton* and *Yeovil*
Bristol (Clifton) — The Cheese Shop
Castle Cary – Manor Dairy Farm (Mr Churchouse) sells cheese and other dairy products
Wyke Bruton – Whitehouse Farm (Messrs Clothier) sells cheese and butter

Delicatessens

Cornwall

Launceston – Folleys

Devon

Barnstaple – Masseys
                  Pepperpot
Bideford – Derrigans
Brixham – Culinarie
Dartmouth – Cundalls
Exeter – Wattys
Honiton – Paveys
Tavistock – Crebers
Tiverton – Greenslades
Topsham – Free Vintners

Torquay – The Delicatessen
Torrington – Jellys

Somerset
Bath – Abbey Delicatessen
   Popjoys (shop)
Glastonbury – Truckle of Cheese
Wellington – Virgin
Wells – Cathedral Cuisine

Drinks

Cornwall
Redruth – Devenish Brewery brews traditionally made beer and sells in a number of licensed houses. At these same houses there are available attractive little maps which show the discerning traveller where else these Devenish beers can be bought

Devon
Exeter — David Baillie Vintners are agents for Wootton Vines
Yearlstone Manor – Miss Pearkes has an established vineyard and hopes soon to be selling wine from her grapes

Dorset
Bridport – Palmers Breweries, traditional beer
Weymouth – Devenish Breweries whose real draught beers – Wessex and Cornish best bitter – are traditionally brewed from the best malt and hops

Somerset
Bradford on Tone — Sheppy's Cider Factory makes and sells farmhouse cider. There is also a farmhouse cider museum and visits can be arranged
Bristol (Clifton) – Downside Wines Ltd sells perry
Shepton Mallet — Pilton Manor Vineyards make and sell wine. Visits by arrangement
Shepton Mallet — (Wootton) — Wootton Vines, North Town House, sell their own wines. Wine-tastings and visits can be arranged
Wedmore – Oak Tree Farm (Messrs Hatch) sells cider
Wedmore – Westholme farm (Mr Banwell) sells cider

Fish

Cornwall
Charlestown – The Cornish Smoked Mackerel Company sells their products from the factory and also throughout the south-west

Devon
Newton Abbot – Youngs Sea Foods process all sea foods and sell locally and nationally

Flour

Somerset
Crewkerne — Clapton Mills sell stoneground wholemeal flour and flour products. Visits to the waterwheel and mill by arrangement
Priston Mill Farm (Mr Hopwood) sells stoneground wholemeal flour and other flour by-products. Also local produce from their farm shop (open daily during summer)

Food Halls

(all these food halls sell local produce wherever possible)

Devon
Exeter – Dingles
Plymouth – Dingles

Dorset
Bournemouth – Dingles

Somerset
Bath – Caters
   Jollys
Bristol – Dingles
   Lewis

Fruit & Vegetables

(farm shops)

Cornwall
Mevagissey — Avalon Gardens

Devon
Marsh Barton – Pic-it-yourself

Somerset
Bridgwater (Huntsworth) — Dawes Farm
(Mr Foxwell)
Cheddar – Axbridge Mushroom Co.
Forde Abbey & Tatworth Fruit Farms —
pick-it-yourself and a farm shop
Minehead – Middlecombe Nurseries (Mr Jones) –
shop and garden centre
South Petherton (West Lambrook) – Lower Farm
(Mr Gooden)
Stratton on Fosse – Red House Farm (Mr Creed) –
farmhouse cider, eggs, poultry and potatoes

Honey

There are numerous individual bee-keepers in the
south-west and good local honey can be bought
at all the delicatessen shops and food halls
mentioned in this directory.

Devon
Buckfastleigh – Buckfast Abbey Shop
South Molton – Quince Honey Farm

Meat

Somerset
Bath (Kelston) – Mill Farm (Mr Cullimore) – meat
and eggs
Bath (Ston Easton) – Home Farm (Messrs Clothier)
Bristol (Clutton) — Clutton Hill Farm
(Mr Appleyard)
Templecombe — Lower Throup Farm
(Messrs Dibben)

Sweets

Cornwall
Padstow – Buttermilk Shop
St Ives – Cornish Candy Shop

Dorset
Dorchester – The Chocolate Shop

West Country Markets

Many West Country towns still have their pannier and covered markets. They are worth searching out, though sadly, some have only a shadow of their former grandeur. Barnstaple, Dorchester, Newton Abbot and Plymouth are all well worth a visit.

Women's Institute shops and market stalls can be found in many towns. Local women bring home-produced and home-made foods which must be of a high standard. They sometimes sell for only a few hours a week and the times can usually be discovered from the Town Hall or Tourist Information Bureau — but be warned and go early as they sell out quickly.

Market Days in the West Country

Axminster   Thursday

Barnstaple   Tuesday and Friday
Bath   Wednesday
Bideford   Tuesday and Saturday
Blandford Forum   Thursday
Bridgwater   Wednesday and Saturday
Bridport   Wednesday and Saturday
Bristol   Each weekday

Chippenham   Friday

Dartmouth   Friday
Devizes   Thursday
Dorchester   Wednesday and Saturday
Dunster   Friday

Exeter   Pannier market open each day in new Market Hall

Frome   Wednesday and Saturday

Glastonbury   Tuesday

Hatherleigh   Monday and Tuesday
Helston   Monday
Honiton   Tuesday and Saturday

Ilminster   alternate Wednesdays

Kingsbridge   Wednesday

Langport   alternate Tuesdays
Launceston   Tuesday and Saturday
Looe   Saturday

Malmesbury   alternate Wednesdays

Newton Abbot   Wednesday and Saturday

Penzance   Tuesday and Thursday
Plymouth   Tuesday, Thursday and Saturday

St Austell   Friday
Salisbury   Tuesday and Saturday
Shaftesbury   Thursday
Sherborne   Thursday
South Molton   Thursday
Sturminster Newton   Monday

Taunton   Tuesday, Thursday and Saturday
Tavistock   Friday

Tiverton   Tuesday and Saturday
Torrington   Thursday
Totnes   Tuesday
Truro   Wednesday

Wareham   Thursday
Warminster   alternate Mondays
Wilton   Thursday
Wimborne   Tuesday
Wincanton   Wednesday

Yeovil   Monday and Friday

Every care has been taken in compiling this list and I have, as far as possible, included only those markets which sell food and local produce rather than livestock. I would ask the indulgence of local authorities, market organizers and readers of this book if I have left out places which should have been included or put in those which should not.

Bibliography

Berry, Claude, *Portrait of Cornwall*, Robert Hale, 1971

Cobbett, William, *Cottage Economy*, London, 1821

Cornwall Federation of Women's Institutes, *Cornish Recipes* Truro (n.d.)

Fiennes, Celia, *Through England on a Side Saddle: The Journals of Celia Fiennes*, Field and Tuer, London, 1888, written in the 1690s.

Glasse, Mrs Hannah, *The Art of Cookery Made Plain and Easy*, London 1772

Harrison, William, *An Historical Description of the Islande of Britayne*, first published in Holinshed's Chronicles, London, 1577

Hartley, Dorothy, *Food in England*, Macdonald, 1954

Heaton, Nell, *A Calendar of Country Receipts*, Faber and Faber, 1950

Higgs, John, (ed. Jack Simmons), *The Land: A Visual History of Modern Britain*, Studio Vista, 1964

Lewer, H.W. (ed.) *A Book of Simples*, Sampson Low, Marston & Co., London, 1908

Moryson, Fynes, *Itinerary of Travels in Twelve Countries*, J. Beale, London, 1617

Quennell, Marjorie and C.H.B., *A History of Everyday Things in England*, Batsford, 1918

Thompson, Flora, *Lark Rise to Candleford*, Oxford University Press, 1945

Tusser, Thomas (ed. Dorothy Hartley), *500 Points of Good Husbandry*, Country Life, 1948

Index